THE REVEREND W D SWEENEY

A Floating Parish

A Floating Parish

Copyright © (Will Sweeney 2023)
All Rights Reserved

No part of this book may be reproduced in any form by photocopying or any electronic or mechanical means including information storage or retrieval systems, without permission in writing from both the copyright owner and publisher of the book.

ISBN: 9781804673522
Perfect Bound

First published in 2023 by bookvault Publishing, Peterborough, United Kingdom

An Environmentally friendly book printed and bound in England by bookvault, powered by printondemand-worldwide

To my wife Minnie and my daughter Natasha.

Contents

Preface		ii
1	Vocation	1
2	Selection	9
3	Basic training	18
4	'A friend and advisor to all onboard'	31
5	Baby Bish	40
6	Once you say goodbye, it's the countdown to hello	52
7	When your home is a warship	64
8	Ministry at sea	80
9	Ministry ashore	91
10	Maintaining the faith	101
11	End ex	108

Preface

I started writing this book sitting in my cabin at sea. I am an Anglican Priest who has served a curacy and a short time as a Team Vicar before following a vocation to serve as a chaplain in the Royal Navy. If you are exploring a potential vocation to become a chaplain, or you are curious about what it might be like, or for whatever reason you are reading this, I hope you find it interesting and valuable in your explorations.

I have spent many an hour at sea and ashore, thinking about my ministry and the journey that led me to become a Royal Navy chaplain. In my explorations during a phase of considering joining the Royal Navy, I found few, if any, books about a chaplain's experiences of serving in a military environment. Therefore, I decided to start writing about my experiences so far.

I started documenting my unique ministry experiences during one particular stint at sea. At the outset, I wanted to write about the events fresh and unaltered in my mind, and to add further thoughts as my ministry progresses.

As I write this, I am still deciding if I will continue writing and, if I do, what I will do with the result. But here lies the diary of a New Entry Chaplain in the Royal Navy.

Will Sweeney

1

Vocation

First and foremost, any Christian ministry should be preceded by a vocation from God, a calling, for it is within the calling from God that we are equipped to do the ministry to which we are called. A vocation is unique to each person. It is a strong urge to do something that doesn't go away, a presence of conviction that continues to build until you decide to follow it's path. For example, I have had two callings in my lifetime, one to become a priest and one to serve as a chaplain in the Royal Navy.

A young calling

My journey to becoming a Royal Navy chaplain started at eleven years old. I grew up as the youngest child, with two older brothers, in the lovely town of Tavistock in Devon. I was brought up going to church, but once old enough to stay at home alone, I was not required to attend church unless I wanted to. Religion was never forced upon me, questions were only answered when asked, but from a young age, something clicked for me.

Growing up, I was taken to church every Sunday and, to be honest, it wasn't exciting. I grew up in a 'middle of the road' Anglican Church (i.e., no guitars and no incense, but traditional hymns played on an organ and Holy Communion every Sunday). I would go to Sunday school and then be taken into church to line up (a bit like in the playground at school), walk with my parents to the front of the church, and a man in some fancy dress would say a prayer for me. Then, I would return to my seat and fidget until it was time to go home for Sunday lunch. So my first experience of church as a young boy was pretty dull...

When I was seven, I was old enough to join the choir. I could have become an altar server, but that looked like it involved sitting around a lot, so the choir seemed a better option than just sitting in the pews for an hour. I joined the choir and started to learn how to sing. At this stage, I began to be bullied at school, 'fat choir boy' was what they called me. They were right, I was fat and a choir boy, but it hurt to hear it. Regardless I continued to sing and even started to enjoy it.

As I grew older, I started to wonder what all this church stuff was all about. I sang all the religious music on a Sunday but still needed to learn what it meant. At first, I even mistook 'Hosanna' for 'lasagne' and so would bellow out 'lasagne' in my treble voice, until embarrassingly, I realised one day I was singing the wrong word (I mean, even before I knew I was singing it wrong, I thought lasagne was a strange word to sing in church).

At the age of ten, something clicked. The music became quite special to me. Watching the priest at the altar breaking the bread was suddenly powerful to me. I started to feel that I wanted to be that person, to break bread at the altar... I approached my parents and said that I wanted to be confirmed. But as I was only ten, I had to get permission from the Bishop (which I did), and then I started confirmation classes before being confirmed a few months later.

I was lucky in that growing up all the priests I interacted with were brilliant. They were loving, kind, generous and honest people. This made exploring the Christian faith and my calling to the priesthood much easier. To this day, I am most grateful to every one of them. I had been confirmed, continued to sing in the choir, despite the significant impact on my popularity at school, and every Sunday I felt overwhelmingly drawn to the altar.

The easiest, and probably quickest, way to explain my vocation to the priesthood is this. It is as if God lit a fire in my heart with a conviction that I should be a priest. Every time I doubted that conviction or decided I didn't want to do it, God poured petrol on the fire, until the fire was so intense that I couldn't ignore it any longer. Eventually, I knew that I needed to be a priest above all else. I declared this to my parents and friends, and I was just a teenager. Over time, my reputation at school changed. I was no longer bullied for being a choir boy but was given the nickname 'Rev'. There was still banter and derogatory comments (good practice for the navy), but people respected my vocation, well, most people...

In my early teens, I met with a Vocation Advisor. I sat down with them and spoke in depth about my perceived vocation. After almost two hours, the advisor agreed I may well have a vocation and should explore it more formally once I was older. I wasn't expecting to be told as a teenager that I could be ordained tomorrow. However, I was disappointed to hear that it would take time.

In my teenage years, I carried on with all the usual hormonal and first-world issues that teenagers faced at the time. I scraped my way through GCSEs and just about got through A-levels (although that was a close call). I 'flirted' with other Christian denominations, particularly the Methodist Church, before returning to the Church of England and finishing school, ready to embark on university education.

A struggle I knew I would always have was education. I was never good at studying, especially exams, and later I was diagnosed with dyslexia. I scraped enough grades to get into university but was never excited about the prospect. However, during this time, I also started to sense a further vocation: becoming a chaplain in the Royal Navy.

I was now 18, and a degree in Theology seemed the next step to ordination. I was in the early stages of the Church of England's discernment process and had been accepted to study a degree at Bangor (*'Bangor not Banger, it's not a sausage'*; as a local once said to me) in North Wales. But to be frank, and in short, it didn't end well. I quickly fell behind in my studies, and after a year, I dropped out and returned home. I was allowed to restart the year, but no bone in my body wanted to.

I would describe that year as an 'off God' year. Why? Well, for many reasons, mainly caused by my own mistakes, as I realised with time and hindsight. However, one thing that was so abundantly clear during my 'off God' year is that, looking back, God was there the entire time and I was ignoring Him.

I returned home and got a job in a care home, then as a temp worker in an office, as a learning support assistant for a year in a private school, and finally as a barman. All the experiences were valuable work experiences and, at the age of 21, I was accepted to study at St John's College, Nottingham (a Church of England Theological College, linked at that time to the University of Chester) although I was accepted as an independent student – degree attempt number three. Three? Yes, three. On returning from North Wales, I signed up to a distance learning degree course and didn't even make the first lecture. I wasn't ready.

I spent a total of four years in Nottingham. By the grace of God, and some bloody hard work, I obtained a degree in Theology after three years and continued for a further year to study a Licentiate in Theology. During my time, I volunteered as a street pastor and very much enjoyed doing it. But, most importantly of all, I met a fantastic girl whom I would go on to have the lifetime privilege of calling my wife.

Training at St John's required a variety of placements, including a hospital and a local church, and one year I opted for a two-week placement with the Royal Navy. I spent two weeks shadowing serving chaplains, including those who had earnt their 'green lid' (chaplains who have completed the incredibly demanding Royal Marines basic training and Commando tests, earning the right to wear a green beret and who serve with the Royal Marines). Although I had a lot of fun with the Marines, this placement confirmed that I was called to a life at sea and not in the field. After my placement, I returned to St John's even more eager to join the navy as a chaplain.

St John's, Nottingham (now no longer in existence) was a conservative evangelical training college. When starting at St John's, I was a 'middle of the road' liberal. However, as time passed, I discovered and explored more Anglo-Catholic traditions and, over time, I became more Anglo-Catholic. Ultimately, I left St John's College, Nottingham, as a liberal Anglo-Catholic.

I went through the Church of England selection process during my time at St John's and was incredibly pleased to have been selected for ordination in 2012. The selection process took around 14 months, the final stage being a Bishops Advisory Panel (BAP). After the BAP, I had a long ten-day wait before being informed that I had been recommended for training and, having already studied for two years, I was only required to do two more years. I left St John's in 2014, was ordained a Deacon at Exeter Cathedral and took up the role of Assistant Curate in St Thomas, Exeter. In 2015 I was ordained priest by the Bishop of Exeter. After my three-year curacy ended, I was eligible to join the Royal Navy as a chaplain. That meant it took seven years of preparation, a time similar to training a doctor.

Curacy

A curacy is a three to four-year training post under the oversight of an experienced parish priest. During this time, you learn the practical side of parish ministry. I did my first baptism, funeral, wedding, and Sunday service and gradually did more, becoming confident in the role. Finally, after one year and a final interview with the bishop, I was ordained a priest. I presided at my first Mass (a significant day for me), and from there I grew in my confidence and experience as a priest. Throughout my curacy, I often said, *'I am living the dream'*, and indeed I was! I was finally serving as a priest in a wonderful community. Life was amazing.

During my curacy, I started to explore military chaplaincy more seriously. Still, I wasn't sure if my wife and I would cope with the separation involved with regular service, especially when our first child was born. Therefore, my thoughts fluctuated between regular service and serving part-time in the Royal Naval Reserve (RNR). I still had time to think, though, as I had yet to complete the three years required to apply for regular or reserve service.

It was late one evening when I watched a TV programme, and suddenly there was a mention of the Police Chaplain. Naturally, I was intrigued and quickly 'Googled' police chaplaincy in Devon. I found a contact and asked if I could meet with someone to hear more about it. After having an initial chat, I asked if I could join as a volunteer Police Chaplain, and a few months later, I did. I did some brief training, was given a staff number, and was assigned the Exeter Victim Care Unit (VCU). The VCU was a group of civilians offering phone support to victims and signposting if needed. They dealt with various cases and my role was to drop in and support the team, usually by offering a listening ear.

I enjoyed my time with the VCU but all the time I was with them, in my mind, I kept coming back to the idea of joining the Royal Navy. At this stage, I was mid-way through my curacy and decided to go on a

'Chaplaincy Acquaint' (one of the first steps in the joining up process).

I spent three days with a group of prospective chaplains and the Chaplain Recruiter, visiting various naval establishments and interacting with matelots (naval slang for sailor). Then, finally, I got to see a ship, and it was on the initial look around that I suddenly felt a deep sense that this was where I was being called to minister. The Chaplain Recruiter approached me on the final evening and said, *'we would like you to apply'*. So that evening, I phoned the recruitment line and asked for an application to join the Reserves. There were lots of forms to fill in, a few informal interviews, and then it came to the medical...

My issue was that although I was no longer a fat choir boy, I was a fat priest. I passed the medical but was told that I needed to lose quite a bit of weight before I was allowed to take my pre-joining fitness test. Well, here lies the second issue... Until now, I had never run or done very much sport. It was simple, I needed to lose weight and get fit if I wanted to join. So, with a sense of purpose, I started the 'Couch to 5K' plan and shortly after joined a gym. I slowly built up my running abilities and the weight slowly started to come off. And then my first daughter was born...

I remember someone once telling me there is never a good time to have a child or a mortgage, you just have to do it. We had the child, a beautiful baby girl, but I had no idea how much life would change. The day after she was born, I got up at 6 am and went to the gym, feeling fine. After that day, I didn't go to the gym for six months. Whenever the opportunity arose, I was just too tired. However, I managed to keep losing weight and was eventually told I could progress to the PJFT. I didn't. There was something in the back of my mind that was stopping me. I could have passed the fitness test, but I kept postponing it. I felt called to serve as a regular (full-time), not a reservist, but in the back of my mind, the prospect of leaving my wife and young daughter to go to sea was something I could never do. Eventually, three years after starting my first Parish in Exeter, it was time for me to finish my role and move to my first incumbency role in Plymouth.

My first incumbency

Initially my first incumbency was excellent. I was a proper parish priest, ministering, growing the church in terms of numbers, and following a lifelong call, but I soon became miserable. Although I adored my time there, I couldn't stay in that environment, I needed to look for something else. In my explorations, it became clear that, although parish ministry was outwardly perfect for me, God was calling me elsewhere. So I decided to re-open conversations about joining the Royal Navy again. After many chats with the Chaplain Recruiter and my loving and understanding wife (who remembered when we first met, when I told her how I felt called to join the navy as a chaplain), I went on another Acquaint. I decided to resume my application but change it to regular service. This decision meant quite a rapid turn of events. Very quickly I found myself talking with my Bishop about my intentions. A few days later, I spoke with the Bishop of HM Forces at Lambeth Palace. I remember clearly the day I told my colleague in the parish that I would be leaving. Suddenly, I felt a huge weight lift from me. After only two and a half years I was leaving a group of people that I had grown to love and cherish so much. I didn't want to leave them, but the decision was right, I knew it was right. Looking back, my time in Plymouth was not a waste. God had used that time valuably. But it was a delay in God's ultimate calling, which is to ministry in the Royal Navy.

The process had officially started. Although I had started a similar approach previously, it felt different. This time things happened fast, as if doors had been flung open. This time it was the right time, and I was ready.

2

Selection

Once you choose to join the military, in any branch, there are many hoops to jump. It doesn't just happen overnight. As my first application was made some time ago, I had to repeat many early stages, starting with the medical.

The Medical

Like my first medical, I knew a few issues would surface again, the first being my weight. Although I had previously lost a lot of weight, I had put most of it back on, and my fitness had also slipped. The second issue would be my blood pressure. I have always been very nervous around medical settings and, every time a blood pressure monitor was strapped to me, my pulse and blood pressure rocketed. The third issue would be that I am red/green colour blind. As a chaplain in the Royal Navy, this is not a problem as I wouldn't need to navigate a warship or handle any weapons (but more on that in Chapter Four).

I remember the doctor being quite short with me and, at the end, he informed me that I had failed my medical (which was not a surprise as my body mass index was too high). I left with the letter and knew I had to reduce my weight and then appeal the medical. Looking at the letter, it said PMU (permanently medically unfit). My heart sank. Suddenly, my world started to crumble.

I needed a chat with the Chaplain Recruiter, which happened very soon after my medical. The Chaplain Recruiter's role is to try and recruit potential chaplains and then to guide them through the process until they start training at Britannia Royal Naval College in Dartmouth. My experience with Naval Chaplain Recruiters is that they are positive and encouraging. They are chaplains who have been there before and know what it is like, so they have a lot of time and understanding. The Chaplain Recruiter immediately calmed me down and said that I could appeal the PMU determination. In the meantime, I needed to get cracking with my fitness and weight loss. So, over the next couple of months, I lost weight, had my medical appeal and this time I passed. I was now getting closer and closer to the pass grade for the pre-joining fitness test.

The next step was a more formal interview at the armed forces careers office. I met with a naval officer who gave me an initial interview and a bit of a warmup for the Admiralty Interview Board. He asked questions about what the Royal Navy does, its worldwide roles, and its recent tasking. This was really helpful as it gave me an idea of what I needed to read up on before my Admiralty Interview Board, which was exactly what it was designed to do.

The next step was to pass an Admiralty Interview Board (AIB). All candidates applying to be Royal Navy officers, doctors or chaplains must pass an AIB. It is a little like a BAP (Bishop's Advisory Panel - as mentioned in Chapter One). At the time it took place in Portsmouth and lasted two days, although now AIBs are held virtually. Before you can go to the AIB, you must pass the pre-joining fitness test (a 2.4km or 1.5 miles run on a treadmill at a local gym), within a target time.

The Pre-joining Fitness Test (PJFT)

I went into a small room and had my blood pressure taken. I was so nervous, I had to have it done a couple of times before they were happy for me to proceed. As I left the room, I saw a priest walking towards me. A man in a black clerical suit stood out like a sore thumb amongst all the spandex and tight vests, he was a Royal Navy chaplain called Matt. Father Matt is a genuinely wonderful, Godly man. I knew him already as he sometimes helped provide cover for services in my home Church. He had come to give me some moral support. I passed... just! Matt had a beaming smile, and so did I. I changed back into my clerical suit and met him for a coffee downstairs. The gym now had two men dressed in clericals, and we got several odd looks. After finishing my coffee, I jumped in the car and drove to Portsmouth to sit the Admiralty Interview Board.

The Admiralty Interview Board (AIB)

The next day I awoke early and started my two-day AIB. It began in a relaxed way, with the usual paperwork and signing in, and then quickly ramped up. You were issued a number, and you were known as that number for the whole AIB process. I was no longer Father Will or Will, I was Number Four. The first day consisted of a mixture of preparation and exercises. I had to do various written exams and learn how to do multiple Practical Leadership Tasks (known as PLTs) in the gym in preparation for some leadership tasks the following day. I also had to complete an uncomfortable oral exam, where you are given a lot of information to remember very quickly and then asked lots of questions. Four of us sat at a table and were given quick-fire questions, *'which member of the party ashore speaks French, number four?'*. I said, *'Ummm'*, the instructor then asked each of the other candidates until either someone gave the correct answer or we all got it wrong, and then another question was asked. I then had to write a brief outline that I was asked to deliver on how I would deal with a complex situation. I mumbled my way through it. I remember someone once saying, 'when you go in for your brief, use the pointer that is provided'. So I did, but I think I looked a bit of a twit doing so...

The exercise scenario started with, *'You are the chaplain onboard HMS Diamond, and you have lost favour with the Captain and so have been sent ashore with the advance party'*. At the end of my brief, I was asked, *'when you get back on board, how would you make up with the Captain?'*. I am quite a comical person (well, at least I think I am) and often use humour when nervous. So, without thinking, I replied, *'I would hope that with all the media attention showing the Royal Navy helping people in need, it would reflect the ship well, and the Captain would be pleased with this and forgive me. Failing that, I would go back onboard and buy him a gin and tonic'*. *Will, what did you say?* I thought. I was thanked by the staff and told that I could leave. As I left, I heard some laughing... They were either laughing with me or at me. I needed to be careful, this was a serious interview.

In between each activity, we had to march as a group everywhere, which was strange, but I managed. You could sit down briefly at specific points to get to know the other group on the AIB - a couple of reservists, a dentist, and a marine aiming to progress up the ranks and become an officer, made up the other group. My group had three other clergy - two going for regular chaplaincy and one applying for the reserves.

The worst part of the first day for me was the gym exercise. Not because of the physical exercise, but the fact that it entailed a crash course on how to conduct the PLT. The staff demonstrated each manoeuvre with ease and pace, but taking it all in was impossible. That night I got into bed and thought, *'Lord, what on earth am I doing here?'*. I felt so out of my comfort zone and it made me feel a little homesick. I eventually fell asleep and woke up early the following morning to the sound of a Royal Marine band playing parade ground music which was blaring from the speaker in my cabin.

The second day happened so quickly and, before I knew it, it was over. We started with the PLT in the gym. Four chaplains needing to conduct a practical leadership task, it was a pure shambles from the start. The task was split into two phases, a dry phase and a wet phase. The task was to get some empty barrels across an assault course, without them or us touching the floor, and we had twenty minutes to complete the course. The instructors lined up at the side, and amongst them watching was the Chaplain of the Fleet, the head of the Naval Chaplaincy Service. We started the task but weren't doing very well. Finally, after fifteen minutes, one of the instructors halted the test, moved us to the wet phase, and told us we had five minutes to complete the task.

From the brief training the day before, I remember that the first thing that needed to happen at the wet phase (crossing a giant tank filled with water) was that someone needed to get to the other side using a rope. In practice, we had all been very poor at this and there was no chance we would complete this task, or even come close to it. Without thinking, I shouted, 'STAFF, IF I FALL IN, DO I HAVE TO GET OUT THE SAME SIDE I FELL IN?'. He responded, 'NO, BUT YOU WILL ONLY HAVE THREE SECONDS TO GET OUT'. I turned around and jumped straight into the pool, thoroughly drenching the directing staff and the Chaplain of the Fleet. I immediately waded to the other side and jumped out. At first, the team looked at me with shock, then the Warrant Officer yelled, 'NUMBER FOUR, YOU WERE MEANT TO USE THE BLOODY ROPE!'. Some of the staff (the ones that didn't get wet) were giggling. We continued the task and almost got one of the barrels across the tank. The task finished a few minutes later and, as one of us 'had fallen into the water', everyone was punished by sitting up to our necks in the cold water before being marched back to the bus. No doubt I lost a few 'points' by jumping in, but I just wanted to salvage things and achieve the task. Looking back, it was pretty funny, although 're-baptising' the Chaplain of the Fleet was unfortunate...

After getting off the bus, we had a brief chance to shower and change back into clerical suits before a series of theory exercises and interviews. For the interviews (the last stage of the AIB), we were all made to sit together in a large waiting room. One by one, we were called in (in order of our allocated numbers, and so I was last) to get a grilling from the panel. At the end of the interview, you were made to wait outside in a different room by yourself, while your scores were added up and a decision was made. For every aspect of the AIB you were awarded marks. At the end of the AIB the marks were all added up and your overall score meant a pass or fail. After the interview I sat waiting for my results for what felt like an age, it probably was as each interview lasted about an hour. My chaplaincy colleagues had gone in one by one and didn't return. I desperately wanted to see them and ask what questions they were asked or how they found it, but the separate waiting room deliberately prevented this. The scoring for each task and the overall pass or fail score are kept secret. To this day I do not know what I scored, I just know my result.

Finally, it was my turn to be told. *'Number Four, follow me please'*. I walked into the large room, where there was a chair in front of a long table with three people sitting behind it. In the middle was the Chaplain of the Fleet, his clothes now dried and looking a little less bedraggled. On one side of him sat a Royal Navy Lieutenant and on the other side a Royal Marine Colonel. The interview started quite gently with the usual pleasantries, *'why do you want to join the Royal Navy?'* and quickly turned into another rapid-fire interrogation (well, interrogation is probably a bit strong, but it felt like it). I was asked a lot of questions. I was in there for almost an hour and a half. On reflection, I don't remember much of what was asked. I would start to finish the answer to one question and someone else would instantly interrupt and ask another question.

Finally, towards the end of the interview, the Chaplain of the Fleet smiled and said, *'we are almost done'*.

The final question led me to talk about how much I love pastoral ministry and how being a naval chaplain would enable me to do so much of it. The Lieutenant, quick as a flash, interrupted, *'you can do pastoral ministry in a Parish, why join the Royal Navy?'* I looked at him and said, *'because, in the Royal Navy, I get to go to sea'*. The Chaplain of the Fleet smiled and the interview concluded shortly after this, and I was told to wait outside. I was eventually invited back into the room, this time to find it empty, except for the Chaplain of the Fleet. I sat down. He looked at me and asked the expected, *'how did you think that went'*. The Chaplain of the Fleet looked me straight in the eye and said, *'Will, your interview answers were textbook'*. *'Okay, that's good'*, I thought. *'But I don't want to employ textbook'*. My heart sank; it was a fail...

The Chaplain of the Fleet then smiled. *'But when you started to open up and even injected a bit of humour, you were brilliant'*. *'Will, you have passed'*. Hallelujah! I screamed in my head, trying to be calm and gracious. *'Thank you very much!'* I said. We shook hands, and I left. As I left the room, I saw the Royal Marine Colonel through a door window who gave a beaming smile, a thumbs up, and a mouthed 'well done'. The Warrant Officer escorting me asked if I had passed and, when I told him I had, he congratulated me. I was walking on a cloud, desperate to phone home with the news.

Eventually, I got into the car and started making phone calls. My wife first and then my parents. When I got home that evening, I had a much-needed fast food meal (naughty) and was welcomed with some celebratory gifts and a few glasses of wine. Words are not enough to describe the joy that I felt. Finally, I had done it. I had passed the selection process for the Royal Navy. The next step was giving my notice to leave the parish and then to start basic training.

Breaking the news

I was on cloud nine in the weeks following my successful Admiralty Interview Board. However, I was told I could not announce it to the parish until after Christmas. This was difficult for me because I wanted to be able to tell my friends and family about my future ministry, and I also did not want to have to hide anything from anyone in the parish. A few times, I was asked to conduct a wedding or a baptism, or asked about dates I was available for other specific events. I had to be either vague and non-committal or say yes, knowing that I would have to change things after the announcement. I hated not being truthful with people, but Christmas came and went. I knew deep down it was my last one in this parish, no one else did, but it felt like one of the best Christmases ever.

A couple of Sundays later, it was 'the Sunday'. I had prewritten a statement to read to the congregation in the notices after the service. I did the service as usual, and then it came to my announcement. I got emotional as I read it because this parish meant such a lot to me. My news was received with a dead silence and several very shocked faces. I had only been there two and a half years and they would have expected me to stay for four years at the very least. On the positive side I could now tell everyone, and it was lovely to hear so many affirming comments and heartfelt congratulations. It struck me how many of my friends said, '*I remember you telling me you wanted to do this when we were teenagers*' and '*you have always said you wanted to do this*'. I do not remember saying much about it when I was younger but, clearly, God had planted the seed long ago.

I finished off the last few months in the parish and helped to steer the parish as we entered the start of the COVID-19 pandemic. And after Easter 2020, on my 31st Birthday, I officially left the parish and the Diocese of Exeter and joined the Royal Navy. The ministry change also meant a house move and, on July 11th, 2020, I said my first goodbye to family and travelled to Britannia Royal Naval College to start my military training. For the next two months, I would not wear a clerical collar, be addressed by my first name (just OC Sweeney), or get much sleep. Those two months would be some of the most physically and emotionally demanding times I have ever faced.

3

Basic training

Officer Cadet (OC) Sweeney

Saying goodbye was hard. It was the first time I had to leave my daughter for more than a few days. This time it was for two months. I was also incredibly nervous. I learned a lot about what would happen during my training and so I knew it would be challenging. In discussions with previous chaplains, the common themes were *'it's no walk in the park'* and *'just play the game'*. Finally, I was dressed in a suit, said my goodbyes, and drove off waving goodbye to the two most precious people in my life, my wife and my three-year-old daughter. I spent most of the journey praying and panicking in equal measure. It seemed to me I arrived at the gates of Britannia Royal Naval College in no time at all. The college would become my home and my world for the next two months.

In the past, chaplains would do a shortened form of basic training alongside other professionally qualified new joiners, such as doctors, dentists and lawyers. They used to call it the 'Vicars and tarts' course. The RAF and Army equivalent course still survives just for professionally qualified new joiners, but the Royal Navy makes chaplains join the regular intake of officer cadets'. Completing the militarisation aspect of training normally lasts around ten weeks. On completing militarisation, the chaplain then skips the rest of the first term and joins the intake ahead for what is part of the normal officer cadets' second term. This consists of familiarisation with life onboard a warship, known as Initial Sea Time (IST). Only on completion can they 'pass out' (a special ceremony where families and friends watch you get inspected by a senior officer or politician and officially become a commissioned chaplain or naval officer).

Britannia Royal Naval College has three terms each year when officer cadets' can join: January, May, and September. I was initially due to join the May intake, to pass out in September. However, due to a COVID lockdown, the college had to close. So, I was added into a Royal Navy Reserve Accelerated Officer Programme (AOP) course instead. This is a particularly demanding eight-week concentrated course for reserve officers who want to do their training in one go rather than spread part-time over two years (it was a highly condensed version of the usual regular training programme). This meant that my training would be reduced by two weeks. But there was also no time for a graduated build-up in levels of physical activity and, from day one, it was full on. I was one of nine chaplains on this course (three reservists and six regulars). This was highly unusual. Normally, a single intake would only have up to three chaplains.

I arrived at the college gate, got my pass, and then went inside to start registration, taking my final steps as a civilian, where I was first presented with my name badge 'OC Sweeney'. I would be treated just the same as any general-entry officer in the Royal Navy. There were no privileges because I was a chaplain or special insignia to show that I was a chaplain cadet, most people would not even know I was a priest.

Initial Naval Training (Part 1) - Militarisation

The aim of the first part of initial training is militarisation. 'Militarisation' takes you from being a civilian to being a member of the armed forces. It involves a lot of physical exercises, drill (marching) practice, self-discipline, and a good many leadership exercises. You are being assessed as both a leader and a team-player from the moment you start training and you can be told to leave at any moment. As a chaplain, I was equally expected to know how to march, maintain a good standard of military bearing and of physical fitness and show I could be militarised. For a chaplain, the aim of going through basic training is not only to militarise them, but to have the lived experience of what everyone goes through to serve in the armed forces.

First, we were assigned our cabin (our little dormitory). I was in a four-berth cabin (consisting of two bunk beds) and sharing with two other potential chaplains. The cabin was small and quite dusty, as it had been a while since it had been used, so we also had some serious cleaning to do. Next, we had a welcome brief, quick introductions to drill and the various directing staff, and then it was time to be issued with all our kit. The rest of the afternoon was spent trying things on, making sure we had the correct sizes and then a lot, and I mean a LOT, of ironing. We were split into two divisions (I was in Gosling Division) and would remain in these divisions throughout our training.

I got to bed around one or two in the morning, exhausted, on the first night. We were up a few hours later, dressed in our 'phys rig' (exercise clothing) and lined up, ready for our first 'period zero'. Period zero is a strenuous morning exercise that takes place two or three times a week, starting at 0600. I was exhausted when I reached the top field, and that was before the hour-long session started. I just about got through it, and the benchmark of expectations had been set. Over the following week, we had lectures, drill, more lectures, more drill, lots of inspections, usually little time to eat or change rig (uniform) and very little sleep. This was all deliberate and I could start seeing the 'game' I had to play.

In the mornings when there was period zero, the first thing my cabin mates would hear straight after the alarm went off was a can of 'Red Bull' being opened in the pitch black. That was me... A can of 'Red Bull' and a 'Pepperami', to provide some energy before the physical exercise. My two cabin mates were Tim and Neil, both of whom were also New Entry Chaplains, and both genuinely kind and caring priests. Next door to us were another three priests, including a Catholic priest called Tom, who led a beautiful Mass. Amongst the challenging times of basic training, there was also a lot of laughter. I am so grateful for the support and encouragement that I received from my chaplain oppos (friends) and I hope that I returned the same support and encouragement.

About five or six days in, I suddenly realised I had not spoken to my family. It had been so manic that I had no time to think. We shared the occasional message, but I had not spoken to my little girl since I said goodbye, so I found a quiet spot to video call home. Seeing my wife and daughter was a boost, I missed them so much. My daughter came on camera and yelled, *'Daddy!'*. Separation is never easy. I needed to remember, and I did remember, that I was called to be here. God called me to this and so would lead my family and me through it, and God did exactly that. That evening, I just laid in my bed and prayed. I asked God for strength for me and my family to get through this separation. I also prayed that God would get me through the demands that I was facing. Whenever I prayed, whatever the situation, I felt a deep sense of peace and comfort. Without God, none of this would have been possible. Although I missed my family so dearly, God gave me peace, and eventually, I slept. I closed my eyes and opened them, and it was six hours later and time to get up for another day.

The training was continuous. There were no days off, not even a Sunday, and no one could put their hand up and say they did not fall asleep during a lecture at some stage during training. However, the days passed and, as each day passed, I got increasingly into a routine and started to adapt. After about two weeks, we were all bussed to Portsmouth to complete a weekend of sea safety and firefighting training. The weekend was great fun but also pushed me outside my comfort zone. We got to do some firefighting in simulated conditions and damage control drills in a large, moving simulator, a whole section of a ship which was flooded with cold water. You hope you will never have to fight a fire or stop a flood for real, but when you spend so much time on a warship, fires and floods are the two most significant dangers you can face in peacetime. The training weekend was also good because we were all allocated a single cabin. This meant I had a bit of breathing space and an opportunity to video call home.

My daughter had settled into a routine at home and she was excited to hear about what I was doing. I was equally happy to hear about her day and to talk to my wife about trivial things that gave me a brief break from the challenges of basic training. After two nights, we were back on the bus to BRNC. The demanding physical training continued, and the leadership exercises ramped up. We took turns to be in command, including the chaplains.

Next was Dartmoor. Dartmoor consisted of practising wet/dry drill (basically getting in and out of a set of either wet or dry clothes under a small canvas), a long hike and more leadership exercises. Like all training, it came and went, and we returned once more to Dartmouth. A warm shower was most welcome. The days continued, we had a variety of lectures and marched a lot (in fact we had to march everywhere as officer cadets (OCs)), the many inspections continued, as did the late nights and early starts with period zeros.

Now we were almost a month in and the dreaded day of the fitness test came. We all lined up and ran up the steep hill to the astroturf. I prayed as I had never done before, not expecting God to make me an athlete suddenly, but just that I could keep going to the end no matter what. The Physical Training Instructor (PTI) yelled for us to go and I started running. I was lapped by one person twice, but I kept going. After a while, I was the only one left running, gritting my teeth, struggling, and my right knee bursting with pain. I was struggling so much that I lost count of which lap I was on. As a precaution, I decided to keep running, and eventually, one of the staff yelled at me, *'Bish! Stop f***ing running!'*. I hobbled back to the PTI. I had passed. One of my chaplain oppos came to me with a beaming smile and walked back to the cabin with me.

The chaplains on my intake were amazing. We all looked after each other, cared for each other, and accepted support when it was needed. We also ministered to the other officer cadets. After all, caring for those we would serve alongside was what we were all aspiring to do. That evening everyone was allowed to drink a few beers for the first time in a month. We had a big party on the top field. There was a beer, laughter, some sea shanties and, blissfully, a lie-in the following morning. Here endeth part one of training.

Initial Naval Training (Part 2) - Marinisation

Part Two of training moved from focusing on militarisation to an emphasis on being at sea and living onboard a warship. The chaplains on the course, and one other officer cadet, were told that we would spend some time on HMS Albion under the supervision of its chaplain, Father Matt (the priest who came to support me when I was doing my pre-joining fitness test (PJFT). One of the college chaplains invited us for dinner that evening, where we had some fantastic home-cooked food and champagne in the garden - moments like this reminded us that we were human and that training was just a brief phase we had to get through. The hospitality of the college chaplain was outstanding, another example of the love and care chaplains show one another in the Royal Navy.

A few days later, we embarked on 'Marinisation' training. These three weeks aimed to give us an idea of what it is like to live on a warship, but also, as chaplains, we would be conducting a form of 'specialist' fleet time, spending a good deal of time with an experienced chaplain, learning all about the practicalities of serving as a chaplain at sea. For the first time we were able to wear a chaplain's rank slide on our uniforms, accompanied with a small white 'cadet' strip below to show that while we were chaplains we were still under training. Walking as a group one morning, a Warrant Officer walked past us and saluted us. We all looked at each other with a look of *'what do we do?'* before we returned a very loose salute. We had to work on that, as we were now recognisably representing the chaplaincy branch.

Onboard our giant 42-berth shared cabin the beds were divided into little 'alleyways' of six bunks each, and I shared one of these little alleyways with a lovely priest, Rob, who also chose a bottom bunk. As we are both Anglo-Catholic priests, below the mirror separating our two bunks we put up an image of our Lady of Walsingham. The three weeks went quite quickly. We spent much time with Father Matt the ship's chaplain, talking about everything chaplaincy, from what to do on day one when joining a warship to our roles when the ship is at action. I wrote so many notes that I must have worked my way through about three pens! I still have those notes today and I referred to them often during my first year as a sea-going chaplain. There was little to do in the evenings and, as we were still trainees, we were limited to two cans of beer a day whilst onboard. The evenings were very relaxed compared to the militarisation training at college, and it was so much fun sharing stories and laughing with fellow priests who had become excellent friends. On the final day, we walked around the large ship and the training officer asked us various questions to test our ships knowledge. We then returned to Portsmouth to complete our final week of training.

The last week of training focused on drill and preparing for our pass-out parade. There was also a lot more academic study. We were tasked to write and deliver presentations and participate in public speaking and debates. On one occasion, the chaplains were assigned to do a presentation on the realities of war and death. It was poignant and an excellent opportunity to raise a tricky but valid subject. After all, death is not unexpected when serving during conflict operations. The evenings in Portsmouth were mostly spent socialising, enjoying excellent food and drink. The general feel was significantly more relaxed than we had been used to and everyone enjoyed themselves. On one of the last remaining nights, we hosted a sort of 'sod's opera' (an impromptu variety show), which was enormous fun for all concerned. I remember consuming quite a lot of alcohol in that remaining week, staying up until the early hours most nights. However, I also had a lot of pastoral chats during this time. It was almost as if alcohol enabled some sailors to open up more and discuss their concerns more easily. Most mornings, the chaplains would gather with the base chaplains and say morning prayer together. The end was in sight. I had almost completed my training and would finally be known as 'Bish' or 'Padre' (the common way of referring to chaplains).

Passing Out

There was considerable drill practice in the few days leading up to our passing out. This involved a great deal of shouting by the drill instructors as we all made lots of minor mistakes. We kept being reminded that our families would be here for this and we needed to do it properly. We rehearsed the parade over and over and over again. When you thought the day was done, we did it again. As chaplains, we didn't have the added pressure of waving a sword about and, once we passed out, we would rarely have to march again. But we still needed to get it right on the day. On the penultimate day, a Warrant Officer came onto the parade ground and gave us the usual 'this is the worst drill I have ever seen' speech. We were used to these speeches by now.

The day before passing out, we were all gathered in the giant drill shed and told that some awards would be given out to specific individuals, based on each individual's training as a whole. There were four awards, including best officer cadet for each division and best officer cadet overall. Three of these awards were voted on by the training staff, the final award for the best officer cadet was voted on by all cadets in training. As we gathered, none of us knew who would win the awards. The prize winner of the first award was announced, *'Chaplain Will Sweeney'... What?* I thought. I immediately turned to my oppo Rob with a confused look and he just smiled at me. There was a massive applause and I didn't know what to do with myself. I had won the award 'Best officer cadet for Gosling Division'. I had no idea how I got this award, but to say I was chuffed would be a significant understatement. The remaining three names were read out, the applause continued, but then I realised that the following day I needed to march solo to collect my award from the Commodore at the passing out parade. Award winners were usually presented with a sword. As a non-combatant that was considered inappropriate, so instead I was given a sword-shaped letter opener.

The following day we all got up early, dressed in our No.1 uniform, polished our shoes like never before and got ready for the moment we had spent two months aiming for. Before I knew it, I was making my final steps as an OC and the command was given for us to go to our duties. We were now chaplains in Her Majesty's (as it was at the time) Royal Navy. I was so grateful for the support of my fellow chaplains, officer cadets and family while going through training and, above all else, God. God had called me to this unique and incredible ministry, and I had made it, through His love and grace.

Often, with the pangs of tiredness or homesickness, or when 'the game' just got too much for me, the niggles of doubt started to appear: *'why do chaplains have to go through all this?'*, I thought. Thankfully common sense prevailed each time. Prospective chaplains must undergo basic training, not least because even chaplains must be 'militarised'. But it was also because journeying through this arduous and challenging training phase teaches us first-hand what others have had to go through. Basic training for the Royal Navy is difficult but not the hardest of courses (the Royal Marine Commando course takes credit for that). Looking back there was not a single day I particularly enjoyed during basic training (although there were some enjoyable moments). But having gone through it, I became more confident as a person and as a priest. I learnt things about myself that I had never realised, and I was pushed to my limits and overcame them in ways I hadn't thought possible. Am I glad that I was given the opportunity to complete initial training? Yes, absolutely! Every time I walk onto a ship, I immediately have something in common with everyone else. I too had to pass basic training before being allowed to serve in Her Majesty's Royal Navy. Now it was time to embark on that new ministry.

The Transition Course

After my passing out parade, I had a long weekend at home to relax with my family before I packed my bags again and headed to the Defence Academy in Shrivenham, a few miles south of Oxford. New Entry Chaplains (NECs) have to complete a transition course to help cement the different requirements between civilian and military ministry. This three-week course was extremely relaxed and was mostly spent in a classroom setting, accommodated in single ensuite cabins and free to go out in the evenings and at weekends we were allowed to go home. During my time in parish ministry, I rarely had a weekend or even a day off. So, for these three weeks, I began to understand for the first time what it was like to have a weekend without commitments and an occasional evening off. On a Saturday, I wasn't rushing around writing sermons or dealing with administrative tasks. I had the opportunity to be with my family, as a father and a husband.

The transition course was taught by an experienced naval chaplain who had served at sea and ashore for many years. Some new entry chaplains attending it had already deployed with a ship. A large group of potential Army chaplains and a few RAF chaplains were alongside the Royal Navy contingent. The Army chaplains did the transition course before heading to Sandhurst to complete their basic training. So those of us who had just finished basic training knew what lay ahead for them and, naturally, there was much jovial banter about the horrors that awaited them. The Army and RAF chaplains were mostly taught separately from us. However, we joined together for morning and evening prayer, meals and the Holy Eucharist. A significant difference between 'us', RAF and Army chaplains is that they hold a rank (I explore this more in Chapter Four).

Before I knew it, the course had finished, and it was time to go home and prepare to deploy. I had noticed during the weekends at home that I deeply missed my chaplain colleagues whom I had trained with. We had been through some challenging times together and formed a close bond. When it came to the last day of the course, I didn't know when I would next see them again. We shared our goodbyes, and I made my journey home, talking aloud about what I needed to pack and thinking about all I had been taught over the past few weeks. Basic training and transition training was now complete. Now it was time to go to sea for my first deployment. After that, all I had to do was pass my NECs Fleet Board, until then I would be known as a 'Baby Bish'.

Basic Operational Sea Training (BOST)

BOST is a package of training that is delivered to a ship and its company at set periods (for example, after coming out of a refit, on a build-up to specific operations, or to prepare a ship's company for tasking). BOST is a very demanding time for a ship's company, with many early starts and late finishes, and it is delivered by a team of FOST (Fleet Operational Standards and Training) staff, known as 'Fosties'. FOST staff are experienced senior ratings and officers who train and test a ship's company in increasingly complex scenarios.

Day one, week one, will see a busload of FOST staff come onboard and inspect the ship and its company, to ensure everyone is ready and the ship is safe to proceed with training. Following this will be a series of training serials and several small and low-level fire and flood drills. After that, however, it rapidly ramps up, and the scenarios become increasingly longer and more complex. If you have never experienced BOST before, it can be quite an eye-opener, but the training is detailed and thorough and is utilised by various Navies worldwide.

One serial of BOST is 'action messing'. Action messing occurs in a war-fighting scenario when it is vital not to interrupt the fighting, not even for meals. It involves every member of the ship's company passing through a feeding station at pace. For a member of the ship's company, it means eating a hot meal rapidly, while standing up. No talking is allowed, and the Executive Warrant Officer (EWO) stands there, telling people to stop talking and to hurry up while keeping an eye on numbers. It's normal during action messing for the food to be piping hot, and there is no time to be picky. It's either meat or no meat, usually with pasta, so you don't have to chew much before swallowing.

Each training scenario is assessed throughout the BOST period, and further training is given if required. It culminates with an extensive inspection of the ship by a senior FOST officer and a significant fire, flood and casualty exercise. If the ship's company are doing well, weekend leave is allowed, which most use to catch up on sleep. However, if you don't do well in any week, then training can go into the weekend. This annoys both the ship's company and the FOST staff, who all lose out on a weekend at home. BOST is an excellent opportunity for a chaplain to be embarked as it's a demanding time for the ship's company, but also an opportunity for a chaplain to move around the ship during the exercises to get to know people better. As relationship building is a crucial part of being a chaplain, BOST is a great icebreaker and a good way to get to know a whole ship's company and build lasting relationships.

Once BOST is complete, a ship will deploy on operations after a short stint of leave.

4

'A friend and advisor to all onboard'

Chaplains are professional practitioners who are qualified religious or belief leaders already working or volunteering in various settings. You will see chaplains in hospitals, hospices, prisons, schools, airports, shopping centres, serving the police, ambulance and fire services, workplaces, festivals or sporting events, and of course, in the armed forces. The role of a chaplain in each of these settings may differ in degree and because of context, but the overarching similarity is that a chaplain's primary function is to support, provide pastoral care, comfort and advise those they serve. Traditionally the chaplaincy model has been Christian-based in doctrine and concept, although this has changed in recent years, with the introduction of chaplains representing the major world faiths and, more recently, humanist chaplains.

In the Royal Navy, chaplains are known as a 'friend and advisor to all onboard'. A chaplain's primary role is to support members of the ship's company. This includes providing pastoral care, advice, spiritual advice, or signposting, all with complete discretion and confidentiality (except in cases of imminent risk of harm). A chaplain is also an advisor and confidant to command, able to report on general themes or issues concerning the ship's company like morale and operational capability.

However, a chaplain must never divulge private conversations without an individual's explicit consent.

I will go into more detail about the role of a chaplain later in this chapter, but first, a little background on how the chaplaincy branch of the Royal Navy is made up.

The Royal Naval Chaplaincy Service (NCS)

In the Royal Navy, chaplains come from any recognised faith or belief tradition, but the majority are still predominantly of the Christian faith. Civilian Chaplains to the Military represent the Jewish, Sikh, Hindu, Buddhist and Islamic faith groups, but appropriately qualified candidates from most of these faith groups are also able to apply to serve in uniform within both the regular service and the reserves.

As I write this, around sixty full-time (known as Regular) chaplains, alongside a growing number of Royal Navy Reserve (RNR) chaplains, serve the 30,000 men and women who serve the UK in the Royal Navy. To be able to apply to become a naval chaplain, you will need to be currently working as a chaplain or qualified religious or belief leader from one of the following Endorsing Authorities: Christian (Anglican, Roman Catholic, Church of Scotland, Free Churches: Assemblies of God, Baptist, Churches in Communities International, Congregational, Elim Pentecostal, Methodist, Presbyterian, Redeemed Christian Church of God, United Reformed); or Hindu, Humanist or Non-Religious, Jewish, Muslim or Sikh.

The NCS is headed up by the Chaplain of the Fleet, aided by the Deputy Chaplain of the Fleet. The Chaplain of the Fleet is the head of the NCS, with functional responsibility over all naval chaplains. They steer the branch and represent the naval chaplaincy service externally. The Deputy Chaplain of the Fleet is responsible for all internal chaplaincy activities, including all operational units and training establishments. They oversee all recruiting, working with the Chaplain Recruiter, training and education, all faith and belief issues and appoint chaplains to their postings. Experienced chaplains can be appointed as a go-to person for advice or guidance on specific matters such as issues of belief and doctrine, and pastoral offices such as baptisms, marriages, and funerals.

Each chaplain comes under the command of their unit Commanding Officer (CO). For example, suppose a chaplain is serving with a submarine or surface flotilla they fall under the command of a senior captain, but also the CO of any ships or submarines they serve on within that flotilla.

Rank

Each of the three armed services has a defined rank structure, which is an integral part of military life and discipline. In the Army, a chaplain enters with the relative rank of Captain (chaplain to the forces, grade 4). Any promotions after this are initially on time satisfactorily served and then on merit. An RAF chaplain joins with the relative rank of Flight Lieutenant and similarly needs to achieve satisfactory standards and then promote on merit. A chaplain serving in the Royal Navy is appointed to the Office of Chaplain and bears no rank whatsoever. Naval chaplains are neither officers nor ratings and are therefore in a unique position in a rank-based hierarchical organisation such as Defence. They are outranked by no-one and conversely, outrank no-one. They have the unique privilege and custom of being able to adopt the rank of the person they talk to. This means that if talking to the most junior new entry Able Rating or the First Sea Lord, an Admiral, a Royal Navy Chaplain can talk to, and be spoken to, on an equal basis.

This has many benefits, but first and foremost, a chaplain must always address the person they are talking to respectfully regardless of rank. As a chaplain roams the ship, they will usually be called 'Bish' or 'Padre' and would typically respond with the person's job title or their name *'morning Bill'* or *'afternoon Navs'* (nickname given to the Navigation Officer). However, it is sometimes inappropriate for a chaplain to address someone by their first name, especially if they are speaking to a senior officer or rating in public. In the Royal Navy ranks and positions of responsibility are earned and all ratings and officers are entitled to be addressed accordingly.

I have always had a poor memory for names and have often only been able to learn the first names of only those I work closely with. When making my way around the ship, I often greet people with the blanket term of *'shipmate'* or *'shippers'* (commonly used amongst sailors) and often simply use *'cherub'* (my favourite). Addressing shipmates by their first name reminds them they are a person. You can frequently go for months on end on a ship before you realise that the Navigating Officer, *'Navs'*, is really called Steven...

Having the rank of chaplain also means that a chaplain is free to visit any mess (living area). However, I have only ever gone into someone else's mess with an invite, as these areas are people's living and sleeping quarters. A chaplain has the privilege, and should make use of such a privilege, of being able to eat in any dining facility onboard. A chaplain would be failing if they only ever ate with officers, socialised with officers, and went ashore with just officers. Yes, a chaplain is victualled and accommodated in the Wardroom with the officers, but not mixing with any ratings or senior rates would isolate the chaplain from most of the ship's company.

A chaplain wears a uniform with a distinctive badge or rank slide and cap badge. When outside and wearing uniform, everyone normally wears headgear (a beret or cap, depending on the uniform). The only exception is if you are at sea or at flying stations (as a beret may blow off or get ingested into the ship's aircraft engines). When wearing headgear, if a chaplain is saluted the chaplain returns the salute, with a *'good morning'*, *'God bless you'*, or something similar (never just *'thank you'*). Some people might not salute a chaplain. I never cause a fuss when this happens, but I will always greet people as I pass and expect something in response, if only because it demonstrates simple good manners.

Adopting the rank of the person you talk to means that a chaplain will rarely need to salute anyone else or call anyone sir/ma'am, except for the Royal family. Likewise, chaplains shouldn't be called sir/ma'am in return. When I first started, I noticed a lot of Junior and Senior Ratings kept calling me sir and, eventually, I began to correct people *'don't call me sir, it goes to my head – Your Grace is fine!'*. I usually got a chuckle and an *'all right, Bish'*. It broke the ice. However, some didn't stop calling me sir and, in the end, I gave up correcting them. For some Senior Ratings calling people sir/ma'am is just automatic. As a chaplain, you sometimes notice a bit of a divide between officers and ratings, and the chaplains role is to be the go-between.

Bearing arms

All chaplains face the ethical dilemma of whether they should be in the armed forces at all. The role of the armed forces is, above all else, to protect the nation but also, if ordered, to kill the King's enemies in battle. The Royal Navy, and the other armed forces in the UK, do not just exist to kill but also have many different roles, such as peacekeeping, providing humanitarian aid, disaster relief and fishery protection, to name a few. Being a chaplain onboard a warship that often encounters threats and could be ordered to go to war, raises the issue of where does the chaplain stand on carrying or using a weapon?

The Geneva Conventions do not prohibit chaplains from carrying defensive weapons. However, it is MOD policy that all chaplains in the

UK armed forces are not permitted to use nor carry weapons of any kind, even handguns for self-defence or preservation of life. This agreement is in accordance with the wishes of the majority of the organisations that endorse chaplains to serve the military. Chaplains are also not allowed to carry ammunition or transport ammunition or weapons to the front line, it is considered contrary to their profession.

Medics in the armed forces are allowed to carry a weapon for self-protection or to protect an injured person's life. However, a chaplain is not even allowed to do this. A chaplain colleague once told me a dit (a story) about when they were in a tricky situation. They were on a platform of a hostile area's coast and under attack. Someone was injured, and someone ran to the chaplain with the injured person's weapon. The chaplain was asked to hold the firearm so that an enemy didn't come and take it and use it against them. Instead, the chaplain placed the weapon on the side of the ship over the edge of the water and they held it there with their foot. They said if anyone came towards them intending to take the weapon, they would kick the gun into the sea. Was this the right call? I don't think anyone could make that judgement unless they were there at that moment...

A chaplain will have many questions over the 'what ifs'. *What if I could save the life of someone in trouble by picking up their weapon and wounding the enemy? Would I even be able to fire a gun if the situation required me to do it?* A chaplain will not be involved in routine weapons training, so the likelihood of successfully operating a weapon in combat is slim. Some chaplains have argued they want to be able how to make a weapon safe if finding one, for example, if they were in a position where a child could pick it up. However, if a threat suddenly rounded the corner when they were making the weapon safe, the chaplain could be seen as a combatant.

So, if chaplains are not allowed to use a weapon under any circumstances, what happens if they come into contact with the enemy? If a chaplain encounters a threat, it is likely they wouldn't be alone. For example, during the Afghanistan and Iraq conflicts, chaplains deployed to the front line often went on foot patrols with the Marines. If a firefight broke out, the chaplain would duck out of the way and stay out of it until it was time to carry on with the patrol.

If the chaplain was the last person standing, or the group they were with was ambushed and captured, then the chaplain, as a non-combatant, should not be classed as a prisoner of war. This is designed to enable a chaplain to minister freely to prisoners of war, and not need to be detained. But, of course, this is under the rules and regulations of the Geneva Conventions. Some hostile environments might involve contact with those who disregard the Conventions.

Where a chaplain might serve in the Royal Navy

A naval chaplain can be expected to serve wherever members of the Royal Navy are serving. Straight out of training, it is normal for a chaplain to go to sea for their first assignment unless they go on to train for the Royal Marine Commando course at Lympstone. My first assignment was to serve as one of the chaplains assigned to Surface Flotilla (SURLFLOT). This meant jumping on and off Type 23 Frigates and some Survey Vessels. My shortest deployment was two weeks, and my longest was four and a half months.

Most ships do not have a chaplain embarked all the time, primarily due to bed spaces and the need for chaplains elsewhere. However, larger ships, like aircraft carriers, may be allocated a full-time chaplain. If assigned to a large ship when the ship sails, so does the chaplain. It can mean up to nine months deployed away (although in a two-year assignment with a capital ship, you would likely only do one long deployment and a few shorter trips).

All other ships, frigates, destroyers, small ships, survey ships etc., will be served by chaplains assigned to the Surface Flotilla. While in a Surface Flotilla job, a chaplain is expected to aim to be away at sea for 50% of the time. A chaplain has some say in their programme (i.e. when they deploy), but it is mainly decided for them by the Flotilla Chaplain who has a more complete picture and overview of operational priorities and activities. A chaplain in SURFLOT is likely to deploy with a ship when completing BOST or operating in challenging situations. Apart from those sea-going roles, a chaplain may be assigned to a training establishment, a naval base, an air station, FOST, a training role, a joint forces role or (once a chaplain has gained many years of experience) promoted into leadership roles. Most jobs are in and around Plymouth, Portsmouth, or Faslane. Still, a chaplain may find themselves on exchange in the USA, stationed in Bahrain, Gibraltar, on the front line (for example, Afghanistan, Iraq etc.) or elsewhere in the UK. Apart from these roles, a chaplain, with further selection and training, can also serve with the Royal Marines, the Special Forces, or submarines.

There is a vast range of assignments, and therefore ministries, that a chaplain can do while serving in the Royal Navy, and this is one of the reasons I was drawn to it. Often the roles last around two years. Ideally, a chaplain will alternate between being a sea-goer and being shore-based, so chaplaincy in the Royal Navy is not all about being away from loved ones all the time. There is also harmony time at home. With assignments lasting around two years, if you don't enjoy a role, you know it won't be forever. If you particularly enjoy a specific role, you leave with good memories of wanting more. All personnel can express their preference about postings, however, operational capability comes first, so sometimes you don't get precisely what you want.

Like all other branches in the Royal Navy, chaplains have an appointer whose role is to move chaplains around, filling the various posts as required. You would think that would be easy with relatively few chaplains, but it isn't. It's a logistics nightmare (like herding cats), and there will always be some chaplains that don't get their first choice or are moved when they don't want to be. But this is a sacrificial ministry and, this is a vocation.

    I explore these areas later in the book, but first, back to the beginning. After completing basic training, I now had a good idea of what a chaplain does and where I would fit within the branch. Now it was time to deploy as a 'Baby Bish' for the first time.

5

Baby Bish

The First Deployment

When I was a newly ordained curate, I felt that I was starting at the bottom rung of a ladder. I was very new to the role and knew very little, but I was also very keen to get going after a long journey to that point. Preparing for my first deployment, I felt very much the same. Having completed all the basic training, I was glad that phase was over and I felt proud to wear the uniform. However, I also felt incredibly nervous. During the chaplain's transition course, I asked all the questions I thought I needed to know the answers to. I had a packing list, and all I had to do was to start packing and, wow, did I pack.

My first trip was scheduled shortly after the transition course had ended, and I was to deploy for approximately nine weeks, including being away for Christmas and New Year. Having always worked at Christmas as a priest, I wasn't too phased by this. Over a couple of days, I had all my kit and other items sprawled out over my bed, checking and checking and checking again that I had everything I needed. Looking back, I realised I had packed too much stuff, but I didn't know this was the case then.

In the end, I had two full grips (issued large black bags) full to bursting point with clothes, books, chargers, toiletries, and everything except the kitchen sink: it was like I was moving house, not deploying for nine weeks.

Having come and gone a few times, my three-year-old daughter was struggling with the prospect that I had to go away again. I decided to ease this by recording bedtime stories for her to listen to. I brought her a teddy bear (if you pressed its paw, she could hear my voice) and made her a countdown calendar. In addition, every Saturday, she could choose a 'lucky dip' present from a bag, which included a number of small, individually wrapped items (mainly from Poundland). She loved little presents and I thought the countdown calendar would help her break the trip into smaller chunks. Eventually, I had everything packed, stories recorded, 'lucky dip' presents wrapped, and Christmas presents sorted (strange to think about that in October). I had contacted the ship and had instructions to join them in Scotland. This meant a very long drive and then I would be required to isolate for two weeks (as it was late 2020 and COVID was still widespread).

It was just before the date I had expected to go, I was preparing myself and my family for my departure, and then I heard that my joining had been delayed for a few days. At first, I was pleased as it gave me a little more time at home, but then I had to start the 'last few days' routines again. It happened again a few days later, with another short delay. The delays meant I was home for my daughter's birthday, which was fantastic. But the constant uncertainty of when the day of departure would come was also tough. Part of me just wanted to go, the goodbyes were dragging out, and it was getting more challenging for us all. Eventually, the car hire arrived, and the next day I waved goodbye to my two beautiful girls and my black Labrador, to start the long drive to Faslane, Scotland.

The long drive was good for me as it gave me the time to process the goodbye and start thinking about what was to come. To say I was nervous was a complete understatement: I was terrified. Eventually, I found where I needed to go, dropped the hire car off, and sat in my small, silent cabin alongside, where I would be confined to quarters for two weeks. The first thing I did was unpack and put photos of my family on the wall. Then I went to bed, asking God, *'what am I doing here?'*. In the following two weeks, I was able to start interacting with some of the other people also isolating before joining the ship. It was my first proper interaction with matelots and, within a couple of days, I had my first knock on the door. *'Bish, can I have a word?'*. The days dragged, the food was horrible (I mean awful), the fresh air minimal, and the only exercise was walking to the sick bay to have regular COVID tests to ensure we weren't infecting each other.

A couple of days before we were due to join the ship (which some could see sailing into port from their window), someone tested positive for COVID. So we had to do another two weeks in isolation. This time, no interaction with one another was allowed. Each person was confined to their cabin and not allowed to leave under any circumstance for another two weeks. We had to wash our clothes in our en-suite shower and occasionally we were allowed to order supplies from the local shop (known as the NAAFI), which stands for Navy, Army and Air Force Institutes. My order was predominantly beer, cheese, and crackers, rather than toothpaste and washing powder.

When the announcement of the additional isolation was made, there was a bit of panic and everyone suddenly dashed to grab what they could for their room. I grabbed a toaster and helped someone else move the rowing machine into their room (in hindsight, I didn't make the best choice). Then again, the countdown clock started to a moment of freedom before joining the ship. Over the following two weeks, I ran some 'Zoom' quizzes for those in isolation and 'Zoom' church on a Sunday, which attracted a few people. Having spent two weeks stuck in a room, another two weeks was a real struggle. Some couldn't cope, so I spent most evenings chatting with the doctor (who was also in isolation prior to joining the ship) about people of concern and, more generally. I used the time to binge-watch Netflix and plan Sunday services. Eventually, we reached the final day, and everyone was excited to leave isolation and join the ship. On the last day, I put on my uniform and heaved all my heavy bags downstairs, where we all lined up, ready to join the ship. An hour later, I boarded *HMS Northumberland*, my new home, for five to six weeks.

As I walked across the gangway, I was greeted by the Captain, an amiable man, before I was ushered into the ship and down a deck for some food. There was frantic activity everywhere as the ship was getting ready to sail and there were a lot of new joiners. Everyone was friendly and welcoming, but they also assumed I knew exactly what I was doing. Afterall I now wore the chaplain's 'rank' slide without the white cadet strip. I had no white flash to signify me as new and inexperienced (known as a 'nozzer'). I was shown where I would be staying, a bunk in a four-person cabin, and I looked on with fear when I realised mine was the top bunk, almost six feet in the air. *'I will worry about how to get in that later'*, I thought. I then started to roam the ship and I felt utterly lost. I had another 'what on earth am I doing here' moment, before I prayed, and God filled me with energy and comfort. After that, I just got on with it, making my way around the ship and finding out how life onboard works. The following few days were a whirlwind, as I attended various new joiner briefs, navigated my way around the ship completing a joining routine, and got used to climbing into and getting out of a top bunk on a ship that rolled heavily.

On this trip, I would be sharing a cabin with the helicopter pilot, the helicopter observer and the 'METO', the meteorological officer. They were all charming people who helped me settle in and showed me around the ship. After a few days, I started finding my feet and settled into the routines. Soon it was time for my first Sunday service. I had printed off about ten orders of service, having no idea how many would show up. When suddenly fifteen people arrived, I couldn't believe it! The service went well, my sermon's theme was 'exploring Christianity is a little bit like internet dating' and, afterwards, we all sat down and had tea and biscuits. The attendance at Church continued and I would also get a few for Holy Communion on a Sunday evening.

As the days went on, I felt more and more at ease. I felt strongly that this was where God wanted me to be and, although I had a lot to learn, I was starting to learn it. I had survived my first sea state seven, where the ship was pitching drastically, and wasn't sick. I loved being at sea. After a few days, I could phone home and, by this stage, my daughter had settled into her new routines: life was good. I haven't mentioned until now that some of the new joiners to the ship were a film crew recording for a Channel 5 TV series. While in isolation, the film crew talked with everyone and wanted to follow a few of us once we joined, and I was one of those selected. The footage was released about a year later and, although not all events were strictly accurate or presented in the correct order, I featured a few times during the series and the work of a chaplain was presented fairly positively (although I was one of those heard swearing occasionally: sorry, Mum!). For those interested, the series was called 'Warship: life at Sea', shown on Channel 5. The work of the chaplain was occasionally featured in series three, which covers one four-month deployment.

Blue lights

The ship I was on was allocated as the duty towed array patrol ship (TAPS). The ship was tasked to detect and track submarines in the North Atlantic. I can't say much more about it or what we did, but it was sometimes quite an eye-opener for someone who didn't know this was a common requirement on deployment in the Royal Navy. When on operations, the ship would be lit with red light and, when tracking a submarine, a blue light flashed, so everyone knew to be extra quiet (I go into more detail about ships' routines in Chapter Eight). Things seemed to be going well. I had settled into life on board, I had done a few services which had gone well, and we were approaching Christmas. I had heard that Christmas at sea was unique, and I was looking forward to it, not least because I would start the countdown to going home soon afterwards.

I say all was going well. All was going well until the doc, whom I became good friends with, told me that there might be COVID onboard. It turns out there was. Despite all our precautions prior to joining the ship, COVID had somehow found its way onboard. The Captain announced to the ship's company that we were to return to base and isolate: *'not more isolation'*, I thought. We returned to base a few days before Christmas, and I spent Christmas and New Year's Eve just fifteen minutes away from my home. The whole ship went into isolation and no one was happy about it. At least when you are at sea, you have a purpose. In isolation, I continued my virtual quizzes and church, and was pleased with online attendance for both. I joined my family via Facetime on Christmas day and continued my pastoral chats with those who struggled over 'Zoom' or on the phone. After another agonising and lonely stint, this time suffering myself from the effects of COVID, I was eventually allowed to leave and go home. The feeling of freedom was like no other. I had been away for nine weeks and had spent just over six in isolation. Later that day, I drove to my wife's workplace and had the first of two hugs I longed for. I stood at my daughter's nursery door shortly after, waiting for the second reunion. We all returned home and, a few days later, had a second Christmas with all the trimmings.

My first deployment was different from how I expected it to be, not least because there was significantly more time in isolation than at sea.

But what struck me the most after returning was how important it was for me to have gone through that isolation. How important to know what it was like to be away from family, who were just down the road on Christmas day. To be truly effective as a chaplain you need to understand and know what those you serve are going through or have been through. I learned first-hand what it felt like to be isolated for so long. I knew first-hand what it felt like to be away from family, cooped up in a room, eating a cold Christmas dinner out of a polystyrene box. It was now that I truly understood what the term incarnational ministry meant.

Although everyone returned home, the country was in another lockdown. I had a few months at home with my family, enjoying every minute before it was time for me to deploy again. I was due to deploy with the same ship, so I already knew some people and how the ship's routines work. Only this time, it wasn't for nine weeks, it was for four and a half months.

Round two

Between my first and second deployments, I worked on the base with the shore-based chaplains and visited some of the ships alongside. Time ashore allowed me to spend some decent time with family, reset, and plan for the next trip. However, the time alongside for the ship's company would be less relaxed. A ship will go through a maintenance package between deployments, so those who don't live locally would get only weekends at home. They would also spend a few weeks at sea doing 'build up', checking that the ship and its company are ready to deploy again. There would also be some changeover in the ship's company, although most from my first trip remained.

Just before the pre-deployment leave began, I took everything I would need onboard and unpacked, made my bed, put up photos of my family and generally tried to make my small space, consisting of a thin mattress and a pair of curtains for privacy, home. I had managed to secure a bunk in a four-person cabin (where I was placed on my first trip), which I would share with the doctor, a Chief Petty Officer (CPO) and a spare bunk that various people would use throughout the trip. I had also managed to secure a bottom, and not top, bunk (much more accessible for my small, chubby self to get in and out of). Once I had everything I needed moved on board and unpacked, I felt a little more relaxed and looked forward to some dedicated time with my family.

The first few days at home were quite relaxed, and then the countdown started. I began to notice changes within me and amongst my family, all part of the deployment cycle (which I go into in the next chapter). The last few days were tough. I almost wanted the day to come to get the goodbye over and done with: I don't like goodbyes. Eventually, it was my last evening at home for four and a half months. After reading a bedtime story, I put my daughter to bed. I then sat with my wife and watched a film. I didn't sleep well that night. I woke up every hour and looked at the clock, five hours to go, four hours to go, three, two, one, 30 minutes... it's time to get up. I had to be on the ship early, so I got up early, showered, and dressed. My four-year-old daughter was still asleep, so I watched her for a few moments, silently prayed for her and gave my wife a massive hug. I got in the taxi and waved at my wife standing at the front door, as the taxi drove away.

The base wasn't far from my house, but I prayed silently in the Taxi. I was so thankful the driver didn't want to talk: perhaps he knew why I was leaving so early in the morning. Finally, I arrived at the base and it was time to switch my mind from dad/husband to priest/chaplain. I experienced for the first time what it was like to join a ship that was about to deploy. There was the customary greeting as I walked across the gangway and navigated my way through the ship to my cabin to drop my daysack, but morale was not particularly high. We were to spend the next two weeks alongside in base port, regularly testing for COVID, before we would eventually set sail on our four-month deployment.

During the four and a half months away, we got alongside and had a run ashore twice, yes, twice. Usually, there would be several stops, an opportunity for the ship's company to relax and 'out pin', but COVID meant that most of the trip was spent onboard the ship. However, much fun was had. Sailors can get creative when they want to, and I had lots of high moments amongst the low ones. Eventually, the days left onboard became single digits, and it was time to return home. I was pretty chuffed that I managed to do a full deployment (known as a wall-to-wall). It taught me that I could do it, but, most importantly, that I wanted to do more. I saw the emotions rise and fall amongst a whole ship's company and in myself. I ticked another country off my 'visited' list and made close friendships.

Task book

You are issued a task book for whichever branch you join whether as a rating, officer or chaplain. Completing a task book encourages you to learn more about your role and demonstrates that you have met specific tasks and are ready to join the fully trained strength or be recommended for promotion. Your first task book is usually completed during training, specifically during IST (Initial Sea Time) – where, as a group of Phase One trainees, you will embark on a ship, go around each department learning about it, and then sit an exam and an oral board at the end of at least four weeks onboard.

Chaplains are issued another task book, the New Entry Chaplain (NEC) task book, which includes nearly two hundred questions and several practical tasks. The questions ranged from how a military headquarters is structured and staffed to the rules about service law and ship etiquette.

The practical tasks ranged from leading a Sunday service to shadowing people around the ship. When I first received the task book, it felt pretty daunting, as there was so much I had to do. You are expected to complete the task book within twelve months and then sit your Fleet Board. As I progressed through the task book, I realised it was a beneficial exercise and I learnt so much, as it enabled me to roam a ship and ask questions. Sometimes the task book was an ice breaker, to chat with people and to have face-to-face time with people who would generally be too busy or a little sceptical about why I was onboard.

All in all, the task book was a good thing to have to complete. I learnt a lot and it gave me the foundations for being an effective chaplain. Eventually, I found all the answers and met most of the practical tasks and, by this time, I had also spent seven months at sea. Then, finally, I wrote a three-thousand-word essay reflecting on my experiences of being an NEC, by which time I felt ready to sit my Fleet Board.

Fleet Board

Having to sit a board is a standard procedure in the Royal Navy. Before promotion or becoming qualified, you must pass a Board successfully. Chaplains sit just two Boards, the IST Fleet Board and NEC Fleet Board. The Board is usually led by the Deputy Chaplain of the Fleet and the Staff Chaplain. The Board is pass or fail, but if you pass, then you are considered SQEP (Suitably qualified, experienced personnel) and can join the trained strength of the Royal Navy. In short, this means that you are eligible for a change in commission (an opportunity for more service in the Royal Navy) and you unlock more pay levels (which would otherwise stop after three years). In addition, you are no longer considered a 'Baby Bish' (i.e. you have some experience and have demonstrated you aren't a complete 'nozzer', with an emphasis on the word complete).

Due to COVID, my Fleet Board didn't occur until I had been in for over two years and I had no idea what would happen during the Fleet Board. I only knew that I had to report in my best (No.1) uniform to the Naval Chaplaincy Service Headquarters (NCS HQ) in Portsmouth. For the weeks leading up to the Board, I kept reading all the questions in my task book. Some were simple and, having done the job for two years, were easy to remember. However, some were quite complex and, as a person with dyslexia, remembering specifics by reading rapidly is hard for me. I travelled up the day before my Fleet Board and stayed overnight in a hotel. I didn't have to report until early afternoon the next day, but I didn't want to risk traffic jams or accidents on the motorway. I checked into the hotel, polished my shoes, prepped my uniform, read the paper, and had a beer (I'm not very good with last-minute revision).

The following day, I woke up early, having not slept very well. I read the questions in the task book one by one, then closed the book and said the answer out loud before double-checking that I had got it right. It was time to go, so I started getting dressed. Everything was fine until I put my socks on. I opened my bag to find grey socks, and my heart sank. Grey socks? What's the problem? Grey socks are an absolute no in the Royal Navy. Uniform states black socks only. Now in a minor panic, I decided to put them on and hope no one would notice - my first mistake. I got in the car and drove from my hotel to *HMS Excellent*, Portsmouth.

I arrived in good time and went to the office where the NCS HQ is located. I was met with a warm welcome and offered a cup of tea. Before I knew it, I was sat in a small office with the Deputy Chaplain of the Fleet and the Staff Chaplain. The Board was formal yet moderately relaxed, and I was asked several questions about my experiences. I didn't find the Board easy, but it wasn't particularly hard: all was going well until the Staff Chaplain commented on my grey socks... For a moment, I genuinely thought I would be told to come back again, but thankfully I wasn't. The Staff Chaplain asked why I wasn't wearing black socks and suggested I could have gone to the shops and bought a pair (my second mistake). In the end, we moved on, but for about fifteen minutes, I felt like an idiot. You may be asking why something as minor as the wrong-coloured socks is such a big issue? It is a big issue. It was a simple instruction that I failed to rectify when I noticed the mistake. On a warship, this can be serious and cause loss of life. I don't mean wearing the wrong coloured socks, although that may be the case if the XO (Executive Officer, second in command) has a thing about socks. If you don't follow simple steps on a warship, like putting the breathing apparatus back correctly after an exercise or incident, or not securing a hatch correctly, then someone could lose their life. If you wear the wrong type of clothing under your uniform, you could be badly burned in a fire. Basic training teaches you that small oversights and simple mistakes can have significant consequences. Not a good start when trying to prove that you can deploy as a SQEP chaplain.

Anyway, enough about socks. The Board lasted about an hour and a half and, at the end, I shook hands with my two colleagues. I was congratulated on passing the Board and left with a huge grin and a 'dit' to share with my oppos, over our next gin and tonic. From here on in, I was no longer a 'Baby Bish' but 'suitably qualified experienced personnel' (SQEP). What lay ahead was a variety of jobs and experiences, a lifestyle, but also the living out of a vocation that I had felt called to since a young age. It was a decision that I have never regretted, a lifestyle that is sometimes demanding, sometimes challenging, always unique, incredibly fulfilling and often very exciting.

6

Once you say goodbye, it's the countdown to hello

The most challenging aspect of being a Royal Navy chaplain is periods of separation from friends and family. When I first joined the Royal Navy, I had a three-year-old daughter and had spent no more than a few days away from her. In my first year, I spent a significant amount of time away, which was challenging yet surprisingly not as bad as I thought it would be. In this chapter, I briefly explore my first experiences of separation and what I have learnt so far, particularly my experience of the deployment cycle before, during and after my second deployment which lasted for four and a half months.

Deployment cycle

Something that every single member of the armed forces will experience in some form or another is the deployment cycle. Like coping with grief, the deployment cycle is a range of emotions experienced at various stages during the build-up to deployment, during the separation and after returning home. Several factors can change how someone experiences the deployment cycle, such as how long they will be away, what will be experienced during the deployment and what they are leaving behind or returning to.

A lot of my pastoral conversations when deployed are linked to the deployment cycle. Not all sailors realise that the deployment cycle is something everyone experiences and is entirely normal. Even fewer realise that, once you understand how a deployment cycle works, it is much easier to observe the highs and lows of emotions that come with it and that knowing what to look out for makes the whole deployment a bit easier. Depending on the deployment length and the individual, the deployment cycle can start weeks before the period of separation starts and it can continue for weeks after the deployment finishes. For members of the armed forces, deployments are a common factor of life, and for some individuals and families the deployment cycle is continuous.

When I first deployed, I didn't know about the deployment cycle and experienced a strong mixture of feelings for the first time. In the days leading up to my first trip away, where I was planning to be away for just nine weeks, I felt a mixture of excitement, fear and panic, and sometimes wished the final days at home away so that I could go. Before my second deployment, lasting four and a half months, I would feel similar emotions and then would feel guilty about wanting to go, not wanting to leave my family but wanting to get the goodbyes out of the way. The guilt was swiftly followed by 'the last' of everything. The last time I would sleep in my bed, the last time I would meet with friends, the last time I would have my favourite meal. It sounds like I was building up to never returning home, but in the cycle building up to deployment, sometimes those horrible thoughts can come into your mind. *What if things are different when I come back? What if my family can't cope? What if I can't manage? What if something goes wrong and I don't come home?* So far in my naval career, I have had to say several goodbyes for varying lengths of time. However, my goodbyes have always been followed by hellos.

One month to go...

I had been through basic training and had passed. I had joined my first ship (part way through a deployment) and had done nine weeks, most of which was spent in isolation due to COVID-19. I had had my first Christmas away from home. But I knew that this was the ministry I felt called to. I had been home for just over two months, with one month to go until I would deploy again with the same ship. But this time doing a 'wall-to-wall', that is, the whole trip from start to finish.

Something I learnt very early on that I had to deal with was the responses of other people. Whenever I met with a family member or a friend, having not seen them for some time, one of the inevitable first questions would be, *'how long are you back for?'*. Not, *'how are you?'*, *'how is it all going?'*, or *'are you enjoying it?'*. But almost always it was, *'how long are you back for?'*. This wound me up the wrong way, and still does, especially as I was once asked this question a few days after coming home from a stint away. *Why do I want to think about when I am next going away?*, I would think to myself. Yes, it was a reality that I would be deploying again, but could I have some time just enjoying being at home, living everyday life, making normal plans, and seeing friends and family, before thinking about going away again?

Perhaps if I told people there and then that I didn't like that question, they would stop asking it. In reality, I would say to them *'about a month'*. *How long are you then away for?* (I start to sigh internally), *'about four months'* (SMASH)... I had just said it. Four months. Until that conversation started, I was excited about being home with my wife and daughter, my pet Labrador, my bed, no pipes on the tannoy system, and no air conditioning constantly whirring away loudly. Now I was faced with the harsh reality that I was again on a countdown to going away. Here the deployment cycle starts.

Everyone is usually either a 'glass half empty' or 'glass half full' person. I do all I can to be a 'glass half full' person, looking at the positives in everything. But, as quick as a flash, then I start thinking of the negatives. The countdown clock begins, 30 nights left in my bed, with my family. Thirty nights aren't too bad, I must not overthink the 134 that will follow. I find that my prayers are more towards my family and the upcoming deployment than my usual routine of praying for the world and those I have encountered pastorally as a chaplain.

Over the following four weeks, my emotions ebb and flow between excitement for the trip ahead, the ministry I feel called to, and the realities of leaving my little girl and my wife at home. I have some productive days, when I plan services and get items packed, and others when I sit and stare at the walls wondering why I am doing this. But, of course, with experience, the deployment cycle gets more accessible. I now know the feelings that I will feel and how to cope with them, how to focus more on the positives than the negatives. But at the time, it was a whirlwind of emotions I was not used to.

Two weeks to go...

Before a ship and its company deploy for a significant period, the whole ship's company will be granted some leave. This is an opportunity to spend time with family and relax. Some go away on holidays, sometimes to quite exotic places. Others stay at home and play computer games or go out drinking with their mates, and some have duties onboard the ship. I decided I didn't want to spend my leave worrying about what I needed to pack and if I had everything, so just before proceeding on my leave, I packed my bags and took them to the ship. I located my bunk and made my bed. I ironed my uniform and hung it up in my locker. I put pictures of my family and friends by the side of my bunk and then took pictures of everything. I am pretty forgetful and, in those moments when I think, '*did I pack that*'? I knew I could look at pictures and see that it was there. If you worry about packing the kitchen sink for a week's holiday, you will understand, only I worried that I would forget something and not have it for over four months. Space on board is minimal, so you must be very mindful of what you choose to take. Some items are necessary, such as a uniform and, for me, church resources. Other things aren't essential but make your life a little more comfortable, such as a laptop and hard drive full of films, books, snacks, and Yorkshire Gold tea bags.

As I was doing a 'wall to wall,' I also loaded on a mattress topper, a proper duvet and two sets of my daughter's bedding, which she chose (a routine we do on every trip, where she chooses two sets of her bedding that I take and use while away). This meant that, for the next four months, I would be sleeping under Disney bed sheets with princesses on. I wouldn't be the only one. Now that my kit was loaded, I could switch off, relax, and enjoy time with my family.

Three days to go...

Strangely, as the time came ever closer, I felt more and more a sense of peace, with only an occasional panic. I had sorted out the important domestic financial matters, recorded several bedtime stories for my daughter, and said most of my goodbyes to friends and family. However, I also started to notice something else, a bit more separation from my wife and daughter. Part of the deployment cycle can manifest in withdrawing from loved ones, which can go both ways. The closer the deployment got, the more I felt myself detaching from those around me, almost to ease the blow of the upcoming goodbye. I wasn't doing this consciously, but now I know this is just part of the build-up.

The final evening...

Before I knew it, I had put my daughter to bed for the last time in a while and was sitting on the sofa with my wife, watching TV. We didn't talk much. First, we sat silently as I sipped my last beer at home and ate one of my favourite foods. Then, as the film filled the silence, we sat together and held each other. I didn't want to go to bed. I didn't want this to end. And then I reminded myself that this is not the end. This is just a brief period of separation, the separation we have done before, and the separation we will do again. I didn't sleep much that night, but it was time to say goodbye before I knew it.

Deployment day one...

I had to be on the ship by 0730, so I woke up early. My wife and I had a coffee together in the lounge and talked as usual. My taxi was booked for 0700, and it arrived five minutes early. I have never been good with goodbyes, I hate them. I was relieved that my daughter was still sound asleep. I went into her bedroom, gave her the biggest hug and kiss, and then stood by her door for a few moments, just watching her sleep, praying that God would keep her safe and that she would be okay without me. I picked up my rucksack and kissed my wife goodbye at the door. I got into the taxi and sat silently until it was time to get out the other end. I sat there and just prayed. When I got out of the taxi, I thanked him, not for the lift, but for not wanting to talk. I crossed the gangway to my home for the next four and a half months and was immediately met with some smiles and sad eyes of my 'flock', my 'parish'. *'Morning Bish!'*, *'Good morning'*.

The moment I crossed the gangway, I felt a little relief. Perhaps it was God's reassurance, maybe the relief that the goodbye was done. I wasn't counting down to going away, I was now counting down to coming home. However, that evening I experienced the biggest lesson I have ever learnt and felt the most profound guilt and regret I have ever experienced.

The first day was quite busy, getting ready to sail, putting my uniform on and getting around the ship. The start of the deployment is one of the busier times for a chaplain. Many will seek you out for one last attempt to try and get off. You encounter those who can't wait to leave (who will also be the ones who will be sad about the deployment ending), and a significant amount of people who are just getting on with it. That evening I couldn't wait to speak with my wife and daughter, I was waiting all day. Finally, my daughter came on the phone and burst into tears. *'Darling, what's the matter'?* She sobbed momentarily before eventually saying, *'I never got to say goodbye to you'...* My heart sank so low that I felt it had left my body entirely. My daughter being asleep meant I could go silently and without causing pain. In reality, I had made a terrible, terrible mistake. I immediately changed the phone call to Facetime and comforted my little girl. I also vowed never to slip away again. I would always wake her up and say goodbye properly.

The deployment

That first night onboard I didn't sleep very well, partly because I still felt so overwhelmingly guilty for making my daughter feel so sad and also because it was a new environment that took some getting used to. However, the following day I woke up and thought, *'one night done'*. I quickly got into the routine of being at sea and, after a week, it felt like business as usual. I spoke with my family as often as possible, and soon the conversations with my daughter changed from tears to her telling me about her day. The phone calls home were such a good morale boost for me and for the family too.

The first few weeks on board were busy, and I mean very busy. I had to deal with many pastoral issues, some of which were quite complex. There were days that I would get into my bunk and sleep like a baby, and others when I would get into my bunk and feel so homesick I didn't think I would cope. As the Bish on board, I was the person everyone could talk to. I would often be asked, *'who do you go to?'*. 'God', I would say, and I wasn't joking. My faith got me through some of the more challenging times; the importance of prayer and taking time out each day was paramount to coping with the demands of being at sea. Due to COVID, we spent a long time at sea without a break. Nine weeks into the trip, we were allowed off for just a few nights. I booked myself into an apartment as a sort of mini-retreat, and it was only when I returned, and someone said, '*S**t Bish, you look like a new man*', that I realised the importance of pacing myself and looking after myself.

Life at sea can, at times be stressful, at times be quite dull, but also, at times be tremendous fun. Sailors can be very creative in coming up with new ideas to have fun and pass the time during quieter periods of tasking. I have enjoyed many a flight deck BBQ wearing a tropical shirt, getting involved with whole ship Cluedo, whole ship quiz nights and plenty of late-night parties in the Wardroom surrounded by inflatable palm trees and loud music. Many times during this trip, I had to pinch myself. I had so much fun that I couldn't believe I was being paid for this. Significantly, these occasions far outweighed the times I felt low or out of my depth. A month in, I felt truly settled. The homesickness still occasionally stung, but phoning home improved it. My wife and daughter had got into a good routine at home, supported by my parents, and I was enjoying the massive privilege of being a chaplain at sea.

Just over halfway through the trip, we had a foreign run ashore, something unfamiliar in COVID times. For me, it was my first foreign run ashore ever. We docked into Iceland and were given four days to explore and let off some steam, and my goodness, the ship's company did. As well as exploring Reykjavik, often by electric scooter, I went out for meals with members of the Wardroom, went to jazz clubs and nightclubs, explored museums, and spent evenings chatting over beers and laughing. I had become close with some of the officers at this stage and it felt like a holiday. We went on a guided day trip as a group, finishing off in the hot springs of the Blue Lagoon. For the first time in my naval career, I experienced one of the biggest highlights of being a sailor, foreign travel.

After a week, we sailed again and continued with our tasking and, once the mid-way point was hit, it was significantly noticeable that coming down the other side of the 'deployment mountain' was so much easier. The total days away were increasing, and the days left before homecoming were getting fewer. Time flew by, and before I knew it we had less than a month to go. Every time I phoned home, we talked about me coming home. It was *'month after next, I am home'*, then *'next month I am home'*, then *'next week I am home!'*. We started to plan what we would do when I was back and we began to talk about everything we would do again as a family. I was so excited, and my mood showed it. However, not everyone was happy. Several people suddenly started to become a lot quieter, a lot more secluded. For some, the goodbye is the hardest, and the prospect of hello the best. For others, going to sea means escaping from issues at home, problems that they can ignore. Coming home for them is when they must start living up to the realities of facing whatever they left behind. During the last few weeks of the trip, my ministry focused on those not looking forward to returning home. Some individuals came from broken homes, others were going through divorce or relationship breakdowns and several sailors would be rejoicing if we were to be extended. As I roamed the ship over the last week, I could easily spot the people who would need support after we had returned.

The final night before we were due home, I spoke at length with my wife and daughter. I couldn't wait to hold them, to be home with them. We anchored just outside Plymouth on our final night, watching the fireworks competition on The Hoe. I joined other officers on the bridge wing watching the fireworks, seeing my home, sipping wine, full of positive emotions. I went to bed early. It felt like Christmas Eve as a child and I was desperate for it to be morning.

Usually, when a ship returns from a deployment, all the families and friends line the jetty. A band plays music and the flags wave, as the ship comes around the corner, with every member of the ship's company dressed in their best No.1 uniform waving back. Sadly, this was not allowed due to COVID (I promise that's the last time I mention COVID). So the ship sailed back to Plymouth as if it had just been out for the day, with no family or big welcome. This, however, didn't stop everyone's, well, almost everyone's, excitement. As we approached the jetty, everyone was ready to go. The gangway was put across and, when leave was piped, there was a whirlwind of people fleeing the ship. Some would have to stay on board and hold duties. I felt for them, but they were mostly in good spirits. Those holding the duty lived far away and wouldn't have been able to return home to come back the following day, but I still felt for them.

I left the base and phoned for a taxi. I was so nervous I felt sick. I hadn't seen my family for four and a half months, I didn't know what to expect when I got home. I had seen my daughter grow in those few months over Facetime. I had heard about all those things that I had missed, and I had not held my wife and daughter in my arms for far too long. Soon the taxi arrived, and I was on my way home. The taxi driver was a chatty man, and we soon came onto the topic that I was in the Royal Navy and was returning home after months away. We went round the corner of my street and I could see my home and my wife and daughter standing at the front door waiting for me. I paid the taxi driver, got out and saw my four-year-old running down the path towards me, screaming, *'Daddy!'*. She leapt into my arms, and we hugged tighter than we had ever hugged before. She clung onto me as we walked back up the road to our house, where I was met with my wife's biggest kiss and hug, and we went inside. I smelt the familiar smell of my home and was pounced on by my black Labrador, who thought I had abandoned him. I sat on the sofa and talked with my wife and daughter, holding them tightly. That night I was able to do my daughter's bath and bed routine, and my dear wife had brought in my favourite beer and food for me to have. I was in heaven.

The next day, we had a family day onboard the ship, so I took my wife, daughter and parents onboard. I got to show them around the ship, where I slept and where I ate, giving a bit of context of what my home had been like for the previous four months. The following weeks were filled with family time, reuniting with friends, and being asked the inevitable *'how long are you back for?'* Being home was incredible but also required adjustment for everyone involved. My daughter, who is usually a fantastic sleeper, drifted into a pattern of climbing into bed next to me every night. My wife, a single parent for the last four months, suddenly demanded more of my attention, especially helping around the house. Although my friends were keen to meet up and make plans, I was utterly exhausted.

During the final few weeks of my deployment, many plans were made, but I hadn't realised how tired I would be or how I would long to stay home rather than go out and repeat the story of what the trip was like. This was another life lesson for me. I would open a cupboard door in the kitchen to get a mug to find rice packets: things had moved, people had changed, and I had to adjust. Of course, it wouldn't be fair for me to come home and expect everything to be exactly as it was, but initially, it was hard. Undoubtedly, it was even more challenging for those I had temporarily left behind. It didn't take long for the first big argument between my wife and me, but we soon settled back into a normal routine.

When I returned to work after two weeks leave, there was much to do. Arguments among couples are common among sailors returning from a deployment. Children had grown, teenagers had changed, and several people had returned to a completely different situation from the one they had left. So my work as a chaplain continued. Within a month, I had already planned my next trip, a six-week trip that would take me to a remote island off the West coast of Africa, to Brazil, the Falklands and then back home in time for Christmas. That second trip felt like a breeze as it was only six weeks and, on my return, I had five weeks leave to move my family and me into our new home, the first home we had ever bought. That first long deployment taught me a lot, not least how I experienced the deployment cycle. But it also taught me that this ministry is demanding, exciting, and sometimes frustrating, but very much what I feel called to.

7

When your home is a warship

As a Royal Navy chaplain, a warship will sometimes be your home. When I first deployed with a ship, there was a lot to learn. For example, I had to learn how to navigate myself around the ship, finding specific departments, and understanding the routines by which sailors live successfully on a warship. Each ship will operate differently; by that, I mean each ship's company is unique. In this chapter, I will explore some of the unique routines and rules encountered when living on board an operational warship.

Navigating a warship by departments

A warship is divided into various departments, all vital for the ship to remain safe at sea and effective in peacetime and in combat. A ship's company is made up of the following departments:
  Warfare
  Executive (including chaplaincy)
  Logistics (including medical)
  Weapons Engineering

Mechanical Engineering

Flight

Each department has a HOD (Head of Department), a DHOD (Deputy Head of Department), as well as Department Coordinators (DEPCOs).

Joining routines

When joining a ship for the first time, you will be given instructions, including which port or jetty you will need to get to in order to join the ship, at what time you can cross the gangway, and what kit you need to bring with you. Once on the ship, you will be given a joining routine, a single side of A4 full of boxes that signify people or departments you need to visit. You must complete your joining routine as quickly as possible once you have joined the ship. It will require you to visit everyone, from the Commanding Officer (CO) and Executive Officer (XO), to have your life jacket issued and your bunk space allocated, to check that you are in date for all mandatory courses, necessary vaccinations and to ensure that you've met all the key people onboard. A joining routine is a piece of paper, so you must start over again if you lose it. You must guard your joining routine with your life. If you leave it loafing (lying around) anywhere, then it is likely that you will come back to find it missing or laminated.

Daily Orders

Daily orders are exactly what the name suggests. Every day, in every warship and in every naval establishment, a timetable is printed and circulated for everyone to read. The timetable will detail every meeting, every activity and any significant movements or visits. Daily orders will also tell you who the key people are for that day, for example, who is the Officer of the Day (OOD), who is the go-to person for each department, and who is the duty medic. Rule number one when on a warship is to read and understand what daily orders say. Why? Because if you are late or miss something, the inevitable response will be, *'it was on daily orders'*. More importantly, you must read daily orders as a chaplain to plan your day, knowing where and when to visit and where and when not to visit. Each morning I am at sea, I will look through daily orders first to identify any meetings I need to attend. Next, I will check that any services I have requested to be put in are there, for example, Morning Prayer or Holy Communion. Finally, I will check if there are any scheduled training exercises or any important visitors coming onto the ship.

Daily orders are really useful. They tell you everything you need to know, including what time you need to get up, what time you will eat, where you need to be and at what time and, most importantly, where you can best minister as a chaplain that day. However, daily orders are also full of acronyms. It is typical for someone new to the Royal Navy to scan the various lines of text on daily orders and have no idea what they mean. For example, CUMDHABFER (clean up mess decks, heads and bathrooms for evening rounds) or RAS (replenishment at sea).

Once you have worked out how daily orders work and what all the acronyms mean, they are a vital tool for everybody on board. Daily orders are also one of two key ways to get information around a whole ship's company. As well as detailing the events for the day, daily orders will have a series of 'parish notices' including social events, competitions, information on upcoming shore visits and, on some daily orders, a fact of the day or some other trivial addition.

The other most common way of communicating information around a ship is through 'pipes', a loud tannoy system that can be heard throughout the ship. Pipes are made throughout the day for specific people, such as the OOD, or for whole ship awareness, such as when colours (the ceremonial hoisting of the flag) are taking place or when a ship's company or department is required to muster. You very quickly learn how to listen to pipes and maintain a conversation.

Learning new routines and naval etiquette

When first joining a ship, apart from learning your way around the ship and navigating the unique acronyms of daily orders, you must also get used to different routines and certain naval etiquette. For instance, you will likely be sharing a cabin with other people. If you are lucky you will share a cabin with one or more others. However, if you are the newest rating on board, then you could be placed in the 45-person mess on a Type 23 Frigate (the name says what it does on the tin, it is a large area with 45 bunks stacked three high). Whether you are sharing a cabin with one or 44 others, the space will be tight, and you have to learn very quickly how to live in close proximity to others.

On my first ship, I was lucky enough to be put in a four-berth cabin and share with others who were considerate of one another. Items typically considered 'everyday' can be considered a nuisance when sharing a cabin. For example, an alarm going off won't just wake you up, it will also wake everyone else up. When you spray your 'Lynx' deodorant, not only will everyone in the cabin get a waft, but the smell could also continue into other cabins. You must be mindful of personal hygiene, ensuring that your towels are washed regularly, and your smelly trainers are not left out.

During my first trip at sea, I quickly learned several ways to be a good cabin mate. Rather than setting my iPhone alarm to wake me up in the morning, as I do at home, I brought a cheap vibrating wristwatch from 'Amazon'. I replaced my thick fluffy towels that took ages to dry with thin, quick-drying towels. I brought several odour balls for my shoes and switched my spray-on deodorant for roll-on, eliminating noise and smell. I learned quickly how to quietly open and close a cabin door or metal drawer so as not to wake anyone up. I did this on the basis that I would expect that my cabin mates would expect me to be quiet, just as I expected them to be quiet when I was sleeping.

When navigating a warship, there are many hatches that you have to climb or walk through. When opening or closing a hatch, you must constantly be aware of anybody coming up, down or after you, as it can be very easy to trap a finger or a hand and cause severe damage. Unlike a cruise ship, a warship doesn't have wide gentle staircases. Instead, it has a variety of ladders to go up and down between decks. It took me a while to learn how to ascend and descend a ladder quickly, sometimes also having to carry a plate of food or a mug of tea. On my first ship, I remember waking up on the first morning and deciding to shower before breakfast. I found five showers and three toilets for about 50 people in that part of the ship. This meant that the rush for a shower in the morning was quite something. A long shower is known as a 'Hollywood' shower and, when there is a queue of people waiting to shower before work, you will very quickly make yourself unpopular if you shower longer than needed. I rapidly learned to avoid peak times and wash later in the day after my gym session. However, it is still essential that you don't take a long 'Hollywood' shower and use up all the hot water.

The NAAFI

The NAAFI is the ship's shop, run by a civilian who deploys with the ship. The NAAFI is often just a small counter, but it is a small supermarket in larger warships. It stocks all the bare necessities you might need, such as shower gel, deodorant and toothpaste, and many things you don't need, but certainly boost morale, including snacks, sweets, chocolate bars and cans of drink. The NAAFI also issues the beer ration for Junior Ratings.

Store ship

When a warship goes to sea, it must carry everything it might need, including fuel, food, parts, toilet rolls and NAAFI supplies. Therefore, there will be a massive 'store ship' before it sails on deployment. During store ship, every single member of the ship's company who is not on duty is expected to form a giant human chain from the jetty to where the food will be stored and, one by one, each item of food is passed along the human chain. A significant store ship can take several hours and can be pretty tiring. However, everyone is still expected to participate, from the most Junior Rating to the Commanding Officer (CO): after all, it is the food everyone will eat for the next few months.

Depending on the length of deployment, there will also be several other small or large store ships according to need. During a store ship, it is common for each sailor to look at what they are passing to the next sailor. *How good are the sausages? How many steaks are we loading on board? How many chocolate bars and packets of crisps have the NAAFI ordered?* All stores (except the NAAFI stock, which is ordered by the canteen manager, known as the 'canman') are ordered by the Logistics Officer, one of their roles being to ensure that the ship and its company constantly have enough food, fuel and supplies to remain at sea for as long as possible. After a few weeks at sea, it is common for fresh fruit and vegetables and fresh milk to run out, so on a long deployment you do have to get used to UHT milk.

'RAS'

RAS (replenishment at sea) is equally important as a store ship. As the name suggests, the critical difference is that it is done whilst at sea. In addition to keeping up a good level of food, it is vitally important to keep up a good level of fuel. Several times during deployment, there will be a requirement to fill up the ship's fuel tanks, which requires the assistance of a floating petrol station, either from a fuel tanker of a friendly nation or one of the Royal Fleet Auxiliary supply ships. The whole process can take several hours, and it is also one of the most dangerous tasks a ship will undertake while not in a combat situation. Due to the danger of the task, the whole ship will be 'closed up' for some time. A majority of the doors and hatches will be shut, in case of impact and flooding, and the CO or XO will be closed up on one of the bridge wings monitoring the task. To RAS, the ship being fuelled must sail very close to the fuelling ship and maintain the same speed and distance at all times, a challenging job.

Once the two ships are in position and the CO is happy, a junior member of the ship will fire a line across to the fuel tanker. Another line is then passed back to the warship, and then the largest fuel pump you will ever see is transferred across the sea and is connected to the ships' fuel tanks. Then the process of transferring fuel can begin. The RAS is sometimes done in rough sea conditions, so constant attention is needed to ensure that both ships and their crews are kept safe. As a junior member of the ship's company, you will likely be standing on the deck getting soaked by large waves, a job I have got involved in a couple of times and now appreciate how dull and cold it is. Once the fuel transfer has occurred, both ships sail away from one another and the tasking continues.

Breakdown of how a ship messes

Every ship is broken down into messes (living areas) and this is done according to rank. On larger ships, it can also be broken down according to the branch in which you work. For example, on most ships, you will have the Wardroom, which is the living and social space for all officers and the chaplain. There is also a Senior Rates mess (commonly split into a Petty Officers' mess and Warrant Officers and Chief Petty Officers' mess) and Junior Rates' messes. Dining spaces are also divided according to rank.

The most significant difference between each mess is that there will be a bar in the Wardroom and the Senior Rates' messes. Although many people on board a warship cannot drink at sea, due to their safety-critical duties, some can drink in the evening or when alongside. Junior Ratings, those with the rank of able rate or leading hand, are limited to two drinks daily. Each member of a Junior Rates mess is entitled to buy two cans of beer or equivalent each day for personal consumption. This is strictly enforced, although naturally, some may try and stockpile their beer ration. However, if caught, you can get into a lot of trouble. The chaplain is victualled as a member of the Wardroom. Although chaplains have the unique ability to visit any other mess, an invitation is still important. For all other members of the ship's company, permission must be sought to visit any other mess. A chaplain may be invited into another mess for specific events, such as a quiz evening, or have a more general invite for a coffee or a drink. A chaplain can eat in any dining facility, and a chaplain should do so regularly.

The CO of a ship is the only person on board who does not belong to a specific mess. The CO will generally have a significantly more spacious cabin than anyone else. However, they eat all meals in their cabin and do not visit any mess without a prior invitation. The CO will routinely be invited into the Wardroom for special events and occasionally invited into other messes. Having individual messes is crucial as it is an opportunity for sailors to be able to switch off and relax. Each mess will have its own mess rules and will have an individual who will be responsible for that mess. For example, the Wardroom Mess President is always the XO and the Executive Warrant Officer (EWO - the most senior non-commissioned officer onboard) will have oversight as the Mess President of the Senior Rates' messes.

As a chaplain holds the unique privilege of being able to visit any mess, the chaplain must have the utmost discretion. When I have been invited into a Junior Rates' mess in the past and have been handed a warm beer (i.e. a beer that has been stashed away), it is neither my place nor is it normally appropriate for me to then raise this with anyone.

Comms

In today's society, young people are used to frequent connectivity, such as using mobile phones at will, accessing Wi-Fi for social media, and keeping in touch with friends and family. However, connectivity at sea is often minimal and sometimes absent. On most warships, there is a minimum bandwidth of Wi-Fi which is just enough to send a WhatsApp message but not much more. Each member of the ship's company is assigned a unique number which gives you 30 minutes credit a week to phone home when deployed. However, it is typical for the Wi-Fi or phones to go down and, with limited numbers of phones amongst the ship's company, it is not always easy to find a phone to be able to ring home.

Once your 30 minutes of free calls have run out, you can pay to top up your phone card relatively cheaply and I do this often, as my routine is to phone home every evening as much as possible. It is not always possible, but part of maintaining my ability to look after everyone else on board means it is essential for me to phone home when I can, as this helps me to look after myself. Most often, my phone calls home are brief and are to check in and say a quick hello. When I am tired or homesick, this dramatically boosts my morale. While at sea, some people have no contact with family or friends. For some, it is easier to get on with the job and not think about home.

Finding a vacant phone or the time to use one is not always possible, and it doesn't necessarily work when you do. On one occasion, it had been a while since I could phone home and I had minimal free time. I managed to get through to my wife and, as I didn't have long, I asked her to put my daughter on the line. The moment my daughter excitedly picked up the phone and yelled, *'Daddy!'* the phone line cut out and I could not re-establish a connection.

For those who joined the Royal Navy many years ago, having Wi-Fi or a phone signal seems a complete luxury. For sailors in the past, a phone call home would often only be possible when in a port and, even then, was not guaranteed. Communication with home was purely done by letters, known as 'blueys' (a bluey is a small piece of light blue paper that folds into an airmail envelope and can be posted free from the UK mainland to any ship worldwide). Although communication at home has improved significantly over the years, it is not perfect. At times, minimal connectivity causes more problems than having no connectivity.

'PED RED'

A ship's specific tasking may require the entire ship to have limited communications. In its most alert operational state, the ship's phones are disabled, the ship's Wi-Fi is switched off, mobile phone SIM cards are taken in, and even emails cannot be sent outside the ship. This strict state is only brought in when it is vital and is often done to protect members of the ship's company or to prevent classified or time-sensitive information from leaving the ship. In these times, anxious sailors who are parents or spouses will approach me, worried that their last conversation with home was negative and now they can't speak with them. The need to 'switch off' from the world can have a massive impact on morale. However, for some, it can bring relief as they won't have arguments about the dishwasher breaking (which always seems to happen when they are away) or hear about everything their families do in their absence. When communications work, and when they don't, differing groups of individuals will struggle and seek out the chaplain.

Different ships and accommodations for a chaplain

Chaplains will deploy on various ships and will be accommodated in various cabins, depending on the size of the ship, the available space, and how long they will be onboard. For example, if you were to join a Type 23 Frigate, as a chaplain, you would expect to share a cabin with three or five other people. On a survey ship, which tends to have a lot more space, the chaplain will likely be given their own cabin, sometimes with both an area to sleep and an area to relax and work, and sometimes with its own en-suite bathroom. A single cabin is a luxury, usually only given to senior officers onboard a ship. For a chaplain, a single cabin helps when meeting with people and having private pastoral conversations and it can also be a valuable space to switch off. However, a chaplain should never expect or demand a single cabin, as it is a privilege, not a necessity. As a new entry chaplain, I have had shared and single en-suite cabins. On one occasion, I was placed in a cabin with a lounge, a bedroom, an en-suite private bathroom and even a scuttle (a round or square porthole). Some chaplains joining a ship for a short period may be given a temporary camp bed in a compartment surrounded by machinery. While this would typically be the case if you are joining a busy ship for a short period, this can be all you have for several weeks at a time.

The newer ships in the fleet may have a dedicated chaplain's cabin and, even if you are deployed with a ship for a short period, a chaplain should be allocated this cabin as it is positioned to be easily accessible for members of the ship's company who want to visit. The space is perfect for pastoral conversations, celebrating services, and even hosting or running small groups. On some ships a chaplain's cabin is located in the same area as the HODs cabins. This means that it can be harder for members of the ship's company to come and find you as they may not want to be seen by their senior officer. Therefore, even if a single cabin is available, a chaplain <u>MUST</u> get around the ship regularly and not just base themselves in their 'office'.

If a chaplain, like most people on board a warship, is not given the luxury of their own cabin, then your bunk is your only personal space. A golden rule on board any warship is never to mess with anybody else's bunk space. My small bunk was my only place of refuge and refreshment during deployments when I was accommodated in a four-person cabin. After a busy or long day, I would lie in my bunk, close my curtains, watch a film, pray, or think about my family. It quickly became a special place for me where I would quickly switch off and, at times, where I would look forward to spending time.

Seasickness and homesickness

The two things you never wish upon anyone at sea are seasickness and homesickness. Both seasickness and homesickness can make your life miserable, but at least with seasickness, medications can help. Perhaps unsurprisingly, a lot of sailors get seasick. In reality, everybody gets seasick at some stage. It's just that some are more prone to it than others. I am very fortunate in that I don't get seasick often and, when I do, it is usually just a short bout of tiredness. However, as soon as we leave the wall, some will have to lie down and ride it out for a couple of days. Every time the ship is due to sail into rough waters, every member of the ship's company is offered sea sickness tablets. Still, few will take up the offer (partly because sea sickness tablets can make you feel drowsy or don't have any effect). I have found that fiery ginger nut biscuits are an excellent way of fighting off any form of seasickness. However, I am also very partial to a ginger nut biscuit, so how much of that is reality and how much of that is a placebo effect, I do not know.

Homesickness is also a common experience among sailors. For some on board, it might be their first time away from home and they could be away from home for months. As a chaplain, I have often awoken or gone to bed feeling homesick, and my response to this is normally prayer. In Chapter Ten, I talk about maintaining faith at sea and how it sustains me while I am at sea. But when it comes to homesickness, my faith and prayer life have always got me through it. As I roam the ship, I often encounter those who are experiencing homesickness. Homesickness, like seasickness, is often short-lived, but sometimes people cannot shake off either. As a chaplain, the most significant warning sign for me is those who never feel homesickness but, quite the opposite, dread not the going away but the going home.

Sea pay

There are perks to being at sea, apart from: travel and visiting places that you might not ever visit otherwise; the adventures; the free prepared hot meals three times a day; the dedicated laundry workers that mean you never have to do your laundry, and the special bonds that you form with those whom you serve alongside. One of those perks is sea pay. Every 24 hours you spend at sea, you are paid an additional sum of money known as sea pay, or 'sea goers allowance'. The pay varies according to how many days you have spent at sea over your career. For example, if you have spent less than 281 days at sea, you will be on level one, earning around £7 extra per day. Once you reach level 2, you will earn around £12 extra a day, and for every 180 days you spend at sea beyond that, you will go up another level, and your daily rate of sea pay will also increase. Sea pay level one doesn't sound like much money, but it's certainly nothing to be sniffed at when you add it up over a four-month deployment. The additional monthly income at sea can also be substantial during your time in the Royal Navy as you increase levels. Sometimes you will hear sailors asking each other which level of sea pay they are on, *'level 4? is that it?'*. *'Level 2?, you old sea dog...'*

The Safeguard rule

The safeguard rule is used during training exercises. It literally guards the safety of all onboard. Before an exercise begins, the pipe *'the safeguard rule is now in force'* is made, which signifies that any pipe indicating an emergency is just an exercise. However, if an actual incident occurs during the exercise, the words *'Safeguard, Safeguard, Safeguard'* are piped to signify that it is an actual event. Safeguard is also a term sailors use to signify that what they say is true. You may hear a sailor say to another sailor, *'safeguard?'*, meaning, are you telling the truth? If you say the word safeguard, you cannot lie. For example, if you are telling your oppo (friend) that the ship has been extended by two months, the natural reaction would likely be *'safeguard?'* If you respond with *'safeguard'*, they will take what you have just said as literal truth, the 'gospel' you could say. If it is later found out that you were lying, you will lose all respect and trust, and possibly have your eyebrow shaved off. Therefore, the safeguard rule is never a joke when used during training exercises and when said to justify that something is the absolute truth.

JCCC

When away from home for any period, there is always a risk that something can go wrong at home, such as severe illness or the death of a family member or friend. In the submarine service, this sort of information is very carefully handled. Sometimes, when the submarine receives a signal with bad news, the individual concerned is informed by the CO or they could have to wait to be informed of such news once the submarine returns home.

A warship at sea, particularly with access to Wi-Fi, WhatsApp, and social media, means protecting sensitive information is much harder to handle. In the past, for example, if a family member of a member of the ship's company were to become seriously ill or die, then a signal would be sent to the ship in the first instance. The individual concerned would be sat down and have the news broken to them (by the chaplain if one is embarked, or by their Head of Department (HOD)). At the same time, arrangements would be made for their cabin mates to pack their belongings ready for them to be sent home. This meant that when the individual was given the bad news, their bags would already be packed and a form of transport would be ready and waiting to take them off the ship and to their home, or to the bedside of their loved one.

Commonly today, it is the other way around. A member of the ship's company will receive a message from home, or see something on social media, and suddenly present themselves to a chaplain or a member of their divisional chain to say that something has happened. This can then start a mad rush to try and work out precisely what has happened, if the individual is allowed to return home and if it is even possible to get them off the ship. Technology, although at times valuable, in these circumstances is well and truly a complicating factor. However, when there are genuine emergencies at home, concerning the severe illness or death of a loved one, I have seen remarkable efforts from a ship to get an individual home as soon as possible, regardless of where the ship is around the world. Likewise, when someone receives terrible news, the ship's company will surround them and support them until they can get off the ship and return home, although humour will still be very much involved.

8

Ministry at sea

Chaplains have been going to sea since the time of Nelson and are not just there to care for the spiritual needs of a ship's company. Chaplains play a vital role in supporting morale and the moral component of operational capability. This means that they support members of a ship's company to remain fighting fit. As well as providing pastoral support and advice, chaplains offer a unique level of confidentiality, and moral and ethical guidance, and can be a useful confidant for the Commanding Officer. They administer the sacraments such as Holy Communion and, in times of war, the last rites.

Until 2023, all commissioned chaplains in the Royal Navy were Christian clergy. However, that has now changed. All the main lived world faiths have had representatives as Civilian Chaplains to the Military in the past, but the Royal Navy is now recruiting suitably qualified non-Christian world faith and belief leaders to join the branch with the prospect of deploying on operations.

Chaplaincy is not about evangelism or proselytising (bringing others to believe a particular belief or faith). Of course, in our roles, we encounter curious sailors who ask questions, but a chaplain does not stand on the main thoroughfare of 'two deck' with a megaphone proclaiming that everyone should believe what they do. Instead, chaplains serve by serving others. Chaplains are called to a life of service, not just to our country but to all those who serve it. The nature of chaplaincy means that a chaplain needs to be a kind, non-judgemental person with at least three years of pastoral experience (because they will need this experience).

A chaplain will offer services of prayer, will lead acts of remembrance and rituals, and organise Sunday services when the ship is at sea. However, aside from this, religion and belief rarely comes into play. In my experience, 95% of pastoral conversations have nothing to do with religion or belief, and the 5% that do are not just about Christianity. I have met with sailors who want more information on paganism, some who are Muslim and need somewhere to pray, and some who are atheists and want to tell me why my faith in God is wrong or ask existential questions that require a philosophical answer. If you feel called to preach what you believe in words and only lead a community of people who believe what you do, then military chaplaincy is not for you.

Pastoral encounters a chaplain might face.

Perhaps the most important role a chaplain fulfils at sea is their pastoral one. In the Royal Navy pastoral care is seen as neither religious nor non-religious but areligious and apolitical. It is "the provision of confidential active listening and support to an individual or group, holding them in unconditional positive regard, while providing impartial and non-directive advice and assistance".

A chaplain must have three years of full-time equivalent pastoral experience and leadership, such as working as a church pastor, priest, pulpit rabbi or in another form of chaplaincy before being eligible to apply to join the Royal Navy as a chaplain. This is because they need to be able to deal appropriately with the variety of pastoral situations they may face, for civilian dependents as much as for service personnel. A naval chaplain is often deployed on their own and, at times, with no communication, so seeking advice is not always possible, therefore, experience is vital.

A chaplain will often deal with sailors who are homesick or want to change branch or get off a ship. A chaplain will encounter sailors whose marriages are collapsing due to separation or infidelity. A chaplain will meet those who are being bullied, are struggling with addictions to pornography, drink, sometimes drugs or gambling, or are in financial difficulties. A chaplain may be contacted by someone who is AWOL (absent without leave). This is a serious offence that needs to be dealt with carefully, the sailor in question often knowing they are in trouble and facing severe consequences. A chaplain will often encounter those struggling with mental health difficulties or problems with emotional resilience, bereavement, or stress at a time of crisis. A chaplain will walk alongside those who must make difficult decisions, such as leaving a partner, choosing to leave the Royal Navy, changing their branch, accepting or rejecting a promotion or extension of service, or pleading guilty/not guilty to an alleged offence. A chaplain must be a friendly face to all who seek them out and remain non-judgemental and impartial, even when faced with a situation they are not comfortable with. They must keep confidentiality and absolute discretion. A chaplain is often required to be a go-between for a sailor and their line manager or divisional officer. On rare occasions, the chaplain is the only person that can go into the Captain's cabin, close the door and have a challenging conversation about the best way forward.

These are just a few examples of what a chaplain might experience during their pastoral ministry. Most of these mentioned I have experienced in one form or another, at the time of writing I have only been in the Royal Navy as a chaplain for three years. The reality is that there will be times when you feel out of your depth and must try to figure out what to do. With time and experience, this happens less often, but the biggest mistake you can make as a chaplain is trying to be a 'fixer'. You won't 'fix' every pastoral situation that crosses your path. At times, the answer may be blindingly obvious to the chaplain, but entirely out of sight of the individual in front of them. On occasions, an individual under a chaplain's care will make a choice that the chaplain repeatedly suggested might not be the best course of action. Sometimes all you can do is listen and be present with a person even if they are in deeper trouble than before.

As a priest, my faith carries me through when life gets tough. However, when sitting with someone with no faith, words of faith are not appropriate or helpful. In so many pastoral encounters as a chaplain, you need to remind yourself that they have come to see a chaplain, not necessarily a religious minister.

Advising command

A chaplain should have a good working relationship with the CO of a ship, and good practice is to chat regularly. A good CO will want to hear what a chaplain has to say, their views on morale or any areas of concern, without asking the chaplain to break confidentiality. A good chaplain will chat with a CO regularly, making them aware of any concerns without identifying specifics or compromising confidentiality in any way. They will also offer the CO appropriate pastoral care and a friendly face, just as they do for everyone else onboard.

A CO is regularly briefed by their heads of department (HODs), informing them of any defects, plans and operational capabilities. In addition, medical officers will regularly meet with the CO and let them know the status of all medical issues onboard. A chaplain will advise the CO more generally about morale and culture onboard but must be careful how this information is relayed. It is not a chaplain's role to dart immediately to the CO's cabin when a concern arises. It is not a chaplain's role to discuss specifics unless permission has been sought; to do so would totally undermine their relationship with everyone on board. A chaplain would typically go to a divisional officer or a HOD for most pastoral matters that need discussion with someone else.

I have mostly kept all pastoral conversations to myself, as there have been no concerns of risk to the individual, the ship's company or tasking. However, on the rare occasion that something very serious has come up, I have often gone to the Executive Officer (XO) or the Executive Warrant Officer (EWO) first, with permission from the individual. In my conversations with any senior members onboard a warship, my advice has often been, *'I would keep an eye on this department'* or *'When was the last time you touched base and dropped in on this mess?'*... You can say things to command without breaking confidentiality, but by highlighting a potential area they should be aware of.

During briefs to command, an individual's name might be mentioned, and this individual might have come to see you. It may be the case that they are being mentioned as there is a serious concern, and you know exactly what their side of the story is. It is not always appropriate to chip in with 'your views' even in these scenarios. I have often remained silent in such circumstances or have said, *'the individual is on my radar'*. If I thought there was a serious risk to life, and I hadn't already raised it with the appropriate people, I would remain silent in the brief and ask to see the CO or medical officer in private afterwards, only discussing confidential matters with those it needs to be discussed with.

Church

Although a majority of a chaplain's role is not outwardly particularly religious or spiritual, church services still take place every week. In fact, it is one of the CO's responsibilities to ensure that a service of worship takes place every Sunday when at sea. There will be a chapel or a dedicated multi-faith space on larger warships. However, on most warships, your 'chapel' is a dining hall or other suitable compartment that briefly transforms into a place of worship. I have often led a Sunday church service at sea on the flight deck in the sunshine, in a dining hall, or conference room. I have led the Holy Eucharist in a tight space surrounded by noisy machines or a vacant cabin. You must work with what you have, which is often not ideal.

Day to day life of a Chaplain

How a chaplain operates depends very much on whether a ship is at sea or not and, if at sea, what 'state' it is in. A ship will normally operate one of three models, depending on where it is and what it is doing. All chaplains will have their ways of ministry in each state, and I couldn't mention them all, so I will briefly explore each state and what I do as a chaplain embarked on a warship at sea.

State 3

State 3 means everyday working routines for the ship's company. Some will be working standard daily routines of 0800 - 1600, but most of the ship will be doing 'watches', periods of 6 or 12 hours rotating between 'on watch' and 'off watch'. When the ship is in State 3, I will start my day by waking up around 0700, getting dressed, saying my prayers around 0730 and then getting to the Wardroom for 0755. I have a quick scan of daily orders and work out what meetings I need to attend, if any, and if any drills or significant activities are happening (such as a man overboard exercise). At 0800, everyone 'turns to', that is, starts work, if not already working. After that, I will hang around the wardroom for another 30 minutes. I do this on Type 23 Frigates as there is no office or single cabin for a chaplain, so I have nowhere specific to go to start my working day. If I started roaming straight away, the ship's company wouldn't have had enough time to switch their computers on, and if someone needed to find me first thing, they would know where I was.

I typically spend the morning roaming the ship, saying *'hello'* to people, and being visible and available. My interactions with members of the ship's company will be friendly and generic: *'What does today have in store for you?', 'Are you looking forward to our run ashore in Amsterdam?', 'How was your run ashore in Amsterdam?'* etc. Sometimes these icebreaker conversations lead to the need for a proper pastoral chat. Sometimes the various discussions lead to a noticeable pattern in specific departments or across the ship (for example, low morale or breakdown in communication – *something to chat about anonymously with the CO later*). Sometimes I will spend most of the day getting around and touching base with everyone. Sometimes, I have roamed most of the ship and it's only 0845. After my roaming is complete, other tasks may come out, such as getting in touch with external agencies, sitting down with other individuals or doing some research. After my roaming and other tasks are done, and assuming there are no meetings, I will exercise (don't be fooled, I do it as a necessity rather than an enjoyment). I will then read, pray, and prepare sermons or services. If it's a particularly quiet day, I will assist in the galley, peeling veg, cooking poppadoms for curry night or asking if anyone wants help painting and chipping the upper deck. Offering practical help where it is needed can also result in opportunities for supporting individuals.

Most days will finish around 1600-1700. But, of course, you can't go home, so I will join others in watching a film or playing a game of uckers. Uckers is a boardgame, similar to 'Ludo', where your sole aim is to 'eight piece' your opponent. This then entitles you to shame them by name on the back of the board with a 'dit' of your victory - a very popular game in the Royal Navy. I might visit other mess decks or research the next port we are to visit, looking at places to sightsee or good venues at which to eat. State 3 is very much a proactive ministry. Some days can be slow, with little to do, and others can swing by with insufficient hours to get everything done. Very occasionally, I will wake up at 0400 and go and stand on the bridge with the watchkeepers or visit those keeping watches in the ship's control centre. I don't do this often as I am not very good with split sleep, but it can be greatly appreciated by those on watch who are bored and fancy a chat.

State 2

A ship will go into State 2 when there is a need for a higher state of readiness. This could be because the ship is in dangerous waters, or because other risks might require a swift and significant response. In State 2, around half of the ship's company will be asleep and 'off watch' and the other half 'on watch'. Different ships adopt different patterns, but each department always has someone up and working. The challenge for a chaplain in State 2 is to be available and present for everyone 24/7. Some chaplains choose to adopt 'six's', the pattern of working six hours and then eating and sleeping for the next six hours, while others will work long days. The pattern that has worked best for me, and seemed to work onboard ships I have served on, is working long days with the occasional late night/early morning roam.

In State 2, I will get up each day at 0600 and say prayers, followed by the morning command brief. I will then do my first roam of the ship and attend the meetings according to daily orders. Shortly after lunch, when there is often a watch changeover, I will roam again and attend the next set of meetings. Finally, I will attend the command brief in the evening, have dinner and go to bed. At any time, at any stage, a chaplain can be 'shook', that is, woken up to deal with something. In State 2, the possibility of an emergency is higher, so I am ready to react immediately to anything that is required of me. In State 2, as much as possible, I get into my bunk after dinner and watch a film before sleeping, allowing myself some downtime.

Twice, sometimes three times a week, I will set my alarm for 0300 and do rounds at night, touching base with people who are on duty. I will stay up until after the morning brief, sleep until late morning, and then continue as usual. It's incredible how quickly it gets around that you were on the bridge chatting at 0400. It is also amazing how many profound conversations I have had in the early hours, as it's quieter and easier to speak with people alone. Therefore, the middle of the night roams are sometimes the most productive. In State 2, chaplaincy is both a proactive and a reactive ministry.

State 1

If a ship is in State 1, then it is at war. The ship will be at action stations, ready to handle the worst possible scenarios. In these times, the chaplain is 'closed up' in the sick bay. Why? They are there to give last rites or to hold the hands of, and comfort, the dying. The chaplain may also be a messenger, reporting casualties from the sick bay to the command posts. Casualty information is never piped over the main broadcast. Hearing your best mate is likely to die isn't good for morale. Instead, the information is written down and passed by hand to those advising the CO on what action should be taken.

The chaplain will also roam in State 1, one of the few people who can. It's good practice to do a figure of eight around the ship, constantly touching base with the sick bay, and regularly reporting back to the sick bay where you are in case you are needed quickly. State 1 is something that many chaplains will only practice during exercises, but it can and does happen for real. Chaplains have lost their lives in past conflicts, and it is usual in a life-and-death situation for chaplains to be required suddenly to offer hope to those who think they will die or know they will. In State 1, chaplaincy becomes a reactive rather than a proactive ministry.

Where might a chaplain serve?

When joining the Royal Navy as a chaplain, your first posting will likely be to a sea-going unit. Usually, this would be on a Type 23 Frigate or Type 45 Destroyer, each with a crew of around 180 – 200, but this can be much more if required. After your initial two-year sea draft, you are likely to be given a shore draft and, if there are vacancies, this could be near your home port. Chaplains can volunteer to serve with the submarine service, primarily deploying with the nuclear deterrent. They can also attempt the commando course, get their green beret, or volunteer to work with Royal Marine units as a 'blue beret' chaplain, i.e. without being commando trained.

For most, you would hope all naval chaplains, serving at sea is the biggest draw. Serving at sea is a unique but enjoyable, challenging, exciting and adventurous ministry. If you are anything like me, then towards the end of a sea draft, you look forward to, and sometimes long for, a shore draft. But when in the shore draft, after a while, you start to long to be back at sea.

9

Ministry ashore

After a draft with sea-going units, which usually last around two years but can vary in length, a chaplain would expect to be assigned to a unit ashore. With all appointments, a chaplain can decide where they would like to go, but it varies heavily depending upon what is available and service needs. After my first sea-going draft, I was very fortunate that a position was open in my home port of Plymouth as one of the base chaplains, which meant that I didn't need to move my family, and the transition from one draft to the other was quite simple.

Where a chaplain might serve

A chaplain can expect to serve in a variety of shoreside establishments. These include naval bases, training establishments and air stations, located all over the country. A chaplain might serve as an instructor at the Armed Forces Chaplaincy Centre at the Defence Academy, as the Chaplain Recruiter at headquarters, with special forces or as a hospital chaplain. Later in their career, could take on a leadership role such as a chaplaincy team leader or become the Chaplain or Deputy Chaplain of the Fleet. Each shore-based role varies in what is expected of the chaplain. Some are predominately pastoral care, utilising a mixture of outreach and drop-in counselling, while others involve teaching and group facilitation. Some roles include looking after a church, so a chaplain may return to a more parochial type of ministry for a stage, baptising, marrying and presiding at funerals and internments of ashes.

Being assigned to a shore-based unit often allows a chaplain to catch up on leave, courses and time at home. However, they can be posts that are equally as demanding and challenging as being at sea. A Phase One training establishment, in particular, is renowned for being a busy 'job', involving a lot of teaching, mentoring and out-of-hours calls when on duty. My first experience of working in a shoreside establishment was being based at *HMS Drake* in Plymouth. I was part of a team of three chaplains who care for sailors who live and work on the base, as well as supporting the team of seagoing chaplains, of which I was one before taking on the new role.

Working as a naval base chaplain

When I deployed on my last trip, I knew that on my return I would be switching from doing my ministry at sea to doing it on land. I would change from a proactive ministry, that required me to wear a uniform and allowed me to explore some unique places in the world, to a ministry that primarily involved returning to wearing a clerical collar and being shore based in an office, offering a far more reactive ministry. I would be lying if I didn't say I was relieved at this stage. I had loved my sea-going time. But I was ready to have a bit of stability with my family, make plans, return home every night, and sleep in my own bed for potentially a significant amount of time.

Having already been based out of *HMNB Devonport*, switching from seagoing to base chaplain was very simple. I moved into one of the three offices assigned to the base chaplains and my first task was to put some pictures up. The offices in DRAKE for chaplains are pretty large. They have comfy sofas, for the variety of pastoral conversations that will take place in them, but they are very bare and otherwise soulless. Moving from post to post can be like moving house frequently, where you don't bother to make it feel like home because you will eventually move on. I can't do this. I need every space to feel personal, whether that is a bunk on a ship that I will only sleep in for two weeks or an office I will work out of for two years. So, I went to 'The Range', bought various large pictures and put them on the large blank walls, to make it feel less like a cell. Pictures were not just appeasing my lack of interest in magnolia walls. They are also, in my opinion, necessary for pastoral encounters. When someone sits opposite me in floods of tears, a picture behind me is sometimes easier to look at than me. It certainly beats staring at the floor.

So, my office was set up, my new role started. What next? As base chaplains on an operational naval base, the sea goers look after all the seagoing units, visiting them when alongside. The base chaplains are ready to react to anyone who drops in during the working day for a chat. Those who come to see us are often sailors, quite often those who are based on a ship or submarine, but the walk to chaplaincy is sometimes easier and more discreet than asking the Bish onboard for a private word. It didn't take long before I started having people knocking on the door asking if I was free. Some days all three chaplains would be working flat out, their doors closed and someone inside each office in varying degrees of distress. On other days, not a single person would come in. You can never tell when it will be a busy day, but it's guaranteed that when you think it will be quiet, there is suddenly a rush of people. Soon I started to have 'regulars', sailors with whom I had built up a rapport and with whom I would be the go-to person for support, just like a parish priest. Or sailors who were going through enduring issues and came to visit once a week, or more, to talk about what was happening.

When you are on a ship for a short time, you don't always have the opportunity to see a pastoral problem through to the end, whereas, on a base, you often do. One of the most rewarding aspects of this ministry, just as it was in a parish, is sitting down with an individual in utter despair at first. Fast forward a few weeks and they are often smiling, and in a completely new, refreshed and happier environment. I do not think that every individual I have seen I have been able to help and it's essential not to fall into the 'fixer' trap. Still, there have certainly been occasions where having the ability to be free, to be ready to react, to have time to be with people, has enabled them to reach a place of greater happiness after being stuck in a position of darkness, for whatever reason. Most of my ministry on a naval base would be this way, waiting for individuals to come and seek out a chaplain, Then we do our very best to help them in whatever way we can, by signposting, listening, advising and sometimes intervening.

So, what about the quiet days? During the quieter periods on base, a chaplain can use the valuable time to catch up on courses. Every member of the armed forces must complete mandatory training regularly, such as: fitness tests; medical and dental check-ups; first aid training; security briefs, and drug and alcohol briefs, to name just a few. In addition, every chaplain must attend a two-day CME (Continuing Ministerial Education) course every year, there are conferences to attend, an annual retreat to take and leave to catch up on. A chaplain may also take on secondary duties for the branch or use spare capacity to study (I have been doing a distance learning diploma in clinical and pastoral counselling, for example). At *HMS Drake*, the chaplains carry out internments of ashes at sea during the warmer months and offer 'pop ups' where we visit ships or units with our 'Aggie's' pastoral workers and provide bacon butties and a space for everyone to get together and chat. Chaplains will be involved in various meetings on base with other care agencies and will regularly chat with senior officers. Similar to being at sea, no two days are precisely the same. It is a varied ministry, and this is what I love about it.

Evenings and weekends

One of my biggest bonuses when working as a base chaplain is the strange concept of sometimes having evenings and weekends off work. You do have these when in a seagoing unit when not deployed. But, like being in a parish as the parish priest, you are always on call, always on the end of the phone should you be needed. On a base establishment with a team of chaplains, you will share the 'duty' of being on call outside of regular working hours. Your evenings and weekends are your own when you are not on duty. I have thoroughly enjoyed the freedom to attend church on a Sunday and sit in the congregation, plan a weekend away with family, make dinner plans with friends, binge-watch some Netflix, and switch off with a glass of wine. Working ashore, I can genuinely be a dad and husband at home. I don't always have to share myself with my parish, worried the phone will ring to interrupt a family meal or there will be knocks on the door late at night requiring me to drop everything. When not holding duty, you know whoever is on duty will answer the out-of-hours calls and react to the pastoral crisis. I have found that I can truly switch off and relax and, when it is my turn to hold the duty, I can return the favour to my colleagues, allowing them some downtime.

There will be times when you are shore based but away from family. Some chaplains and their families decide to move as a family every time they move, some choose to keep the family in one place and the chaplain moves alone, commuting home at weekends. The best choice will vary from chaplain to chaplain. Either way, chaplaincy allows you periods where you can have dedicated family time, which is only sometimes possible in a busy parish.

Duty on-call Chaplain

I have mentioned being the duty chaplain, but what does that mean? One chaplain will be on-call, responsible for the whole local area. In addition, there will be a specific out-of-hours phone number that anyone can ring at any time, which will be diverted to the chaplain on-call. The duty chaplain provides pastoral support and crisis intervention 24/7, three hundred and sixty-five days a year. A shared duty amongst a chaplaincy team means that you may be on-call for several days a month and, in some places alternate weeks.

The key for the chaplain on duty is that they are capable of driving, so should abstain from alcohol, as they could be called out at any time, day or night. They must also be within one hour recall of the base and able to get wherever they are needed within a reasonable time. When I have been duty chaplain, I have had weeks where I have not had a single phone call, weeks where I have had phone calls in the early evening asking about baptisms or to book an appointment for the next day and, sometimes, occasions where I have had a call in the middle of the night, requiring me to get to the local police station or get on base as soon as possible.

Just like base ministry, holding the duty is a reactive ministry and at times it can be pretty busy. At other times, you won't have a single call. I remember being at my parents' house one Friday evening (within the one-hour recall zone). I joked at 2200 that I won't get a call now, only to have a call 30 minutes later from a sailor who lived on site and had just been told that a close family member had died, and they were distraught. This call required me to go on base and sit with them until beyond midnight, having a cup of tea and talking it all through. The next day (a Saturday), I had to liaise with the divisional chain and get compassionate leave authorised so they could go home, and then work out how to get them home as they didn't drive. On a separate occasion, I had a call out to meet with someone who was very vulnerable and needed someone to look after them until arrangements were made to have them cared for. At times I have had calls that simply required a chat over the phone to give advice.

The other significant task you may be required to undertake as a chaplain on duty is kin forming.

Kin forming

When a sailor dies or becomes very seriously ill, the process of informing their next of kin and family is very quickly put into place. For example, a sailor might die in combat, become seriously injured after falling down a ladder chain at sea, or be killed in a road traffic collision while riding their motorbike on leave. In these circumstances, their immediate next of kin (NOK) will be informed, in person, as quickly as possible.

In the case of a kin form, the JCCC (Joint Casualty Compassionate Cell) is informed, and they will stand up a Casualty Notification Officer (CNO) and a chaplain. The CNO and the selected chaplain will generally be the nearest people to where the NOK lives. The priority here is to inform the NOK before they find out by other means (can you imagine seeing on social media that your child or spouse was involved in an accident?). When a chaplain gets the call to kin form, they must respond immediately, even at three o'clock in the morning. A chaplain will normally wear a clerical suit or equivilent, and the CNO will wear their No.1 uniform. The officer and the chaplain will meet up as soon as possible, confirm the details of what has happened and what the NOK will be told (nothing is said unless it is confirmed – if the cause of death is not known, or how they died is not confirmed, then no guesses or opinions are made). Then, the chaplain and the CNO travel separately to the address and will knock on the door together. The CNO will identify they have the right individual, ask to come inside, break the news, and leave when appropriate, allowing the chaplain to remain as long as is necessary to provide pastoral support for the next of kin and family.

During the clonflicts in Afghanistan and Iraq, kin forming was more regular than you would hope it would be. It became a common fear for families that their doorbell would ring one day, and they would see a chaplain and an officer in uniform. Before anything was said, they knew what was coming. One chaplain told me about a kin form he did to a spouse of someone killed in action. As he got out of the car and approached the quarter accompanied by the CNO in uniform, all the mums in the road stood on their doorsteps, knowing what was about to happen, ready to come and support the wife who was about to be told her husband would never be coming home. Kin forming is one of the most challenging roles a chaplain can do and one of the most important – even more of a reason not to drink alcohol when on duty.

My first kin form

It was a typical day at the office, I was duty and making a cup of tea. An officer came in asking to see the duty chaplain. It was a kin form. It would be my first kin form in the Royal Navy. A sailor had died, and we had to go and visit the wife to tell her the bad news. Time was of the essence. I didn't have much time to think about what was coming. An experienced colleague asked if I was ready, and he gave me a way out. If I wanted him to, he would go in my place. I have always felt that there is never a good time for a first of anything and so, although very grateful for the offer, I told him I wanted to go. I sat down with the CNO and discussed the situation, who we would see and what would be said. We agreed that once the news had been delivered, I would give the CNO a nod when I thought they should go (having delivered the heartbreaking news it can be best for the CNO to leave). However, as a chaplain, it is essential not to put yourself in a vulnerable position by remaining in a home alone with a vulnerable person, so you must make careful decisions in each scenario.

We took separate cars and parked down the road from the address. As I parked, I prayed for the individual we were about to speak to and the CNO who would break the news. We walked up a street and, thankfully, there were no pedestrians. We identified the house, and the CNO rang the doorbell. At this moment, I knew we were about to change someone's life entirely and for the worse. The door was answered and the CNO checked if we had the right individual. We were invited in, and the wife seemed confused about what was happening, flicking her eyes between a priest and someone in their best uniform. The individual's name was confirmed, we had the correct address and the right person. Then, the CNO said the dreaded words, *'I am afraid to say that 'X' died this morning'*. You may think it sounds harsh and sudden, but it needs to be. There can be no room for uncertainty. You can't say, *'they have passed away'* or *'they have gone to a better place'*. The next of kin needs to know that the person in question has died or they are seriously ill and, if seriously ill, how long they will have left before they will die.

As the CNO said these words, the wife screamed and collapsed to the floor. I could do nothing but stand there, it wasn't my time to intervene yet. After what felt like hours, but was probably minutes, the wife asked us to sit down and we spoke about what had happened. I felt useless, I couldn't think of anything to say that would provide any form of hope or help in that moment, and that is because there were no words I could say. As a parish priest, I would offer prayers, but not here, and that wouldn't have been appropriate unless asked. As a parish priest, I would have spoken about peace and the individual being with our Lord, but not here. I talked about what would happen next and offered some words of comfort, as best as possible. I listened, tried to answer some of her questions and, just before leaving, gave them my contact details and asked if I could contact them the next day. The CNO and I stayed for about 30 minutes and then left together, as a friend arrived. As the CNO and I went, the streets were much busier with people walking, and everyone looked at us with sympathy and concern, as if they knew what we had just done. That evening I decided I needed to take some time alone. I ate a meal, spent time on my own in reflection and prayer, and the next morning woke up and started a fresh new day.

In the following weeks, I would occasionally ring the sailor's wife, asking if I could do anything to support her, which was often just a chat. I also touched base with the CNO, asking how they were. They said they were fine. I said I was fine when asked, but we both knew that, at first, neither of us was telling the truth. I spent a lot of time reflecting on that event and have since processed it through prayer and reflection. The armed forces require much sacrifice from those who serve away from home and, arguably, sometimes from those who stay behind. My first experience of kin forming was harrowing but also valuable as, when called upon to do it again, I know what to expect. I know what I can do to help and what I can't. I know that in those moments God goes before me, with me and most importantly after me.

10

Maintaining the faith

When I was eleven years old, I started to feel a vocation to become a priest. I remember sitting in my church watching the priest celebrate the Holy Eucharist and feeling so drawn to stand in his place and do the same. I have always loved people, taking a genuine interest in who they are and where they are from, and so I have loved offering pastoral care. When I was sixteen, I started to feel a vocation to become a Royal Navy Chaplain, drawn to the sea, inspired by the opportunity to serve God by serving others in such a unique setting. Although I loved being in parish ministry, I struggled with the amount of administration expected and required of a Parish Priest. I needed to do more pastoral visiting and, when I did, it was short-lived as a meeting would be around the corner, or my time would be needed elsewhere, such as filling in applications for building works.

What I valued most in my ministry as a Parish Priest was saying Mass in a beautiful ancient building, surrounded by candles and the smell of incense. In my last parish, you could be forgiven for thinking it was a Catholic church because our worship was very similar. Candles offer the only presence of light, the smell of incense and the sung liturgy marking the importance and significance of what you are doing. Joining the Royal

Navy as a chaplain meant that I had to strip back to the very basics of the most valued and concrete aspects of my priestly ministry. This has undoubtedly been a sacrifice and, at times, a struggle for me. However, I have also developed my spirituality significantly due to needing to adapt how I worship and pray.

When your altar is a dining table

As I have said before, as a chaplain, you most often deal with the non-religious or those of other faiths and beliefs. For some, leading an act of worship in simple settings such as a dining hall is not too dissimilar from their standard practice. But as an Anglo-Catholic, the Mass is a very significant and essential part of my vocation as a priest. Celebrating the feasts of Christmas and Easter in such simple ways is very poignant but has sometimes been 'not enough' for me.

Church, a physical building, was not a part of early Christianity. In fact, I think I am right in saying that it wasn't until almost 1000 years after the death and resurrection of Christ that physical buildings were used. Initially, the Church was a group of people coming together to pray, worship and hear the priest's teaching. So surely going back to such a way of ministry is more authentic? Perhaps, by removing the vestments, stained glass windows, organ music and choirs, this is closer to the early Church in some ways. Perhaps I have grown accustomed to a bit of 'pomp and ceremony'. However, the vestments, the singing, the incense, the stained glass windows, and the organ bellowing remind me that I am in God's house and not participating in the ordinary but the extraordinary.

The Holy Eucharist, in its simplest forms, can be most profound. I remember my visit to the Holy Land as a curate. We celebrated Mass in the middle of nowhere, using some bricks and corrugated steel as a makeshift altar, which was an incredibly moving and memorable occasion. However, it is not the setting that makes the Holy Eucharist so special, it is the presence of God, Jesus Christ and the Holy Spirit. I have truly felt God's presence at its fullest when celebrating the Eucharist at sea, where I have had to blue tack the paten (the silver plate on which the bread is placed) to the table and cover the chalice with cling film to stop everything going everywhere due to rough seas. However, I have often yearned for the familiar setting I have been used to. Like a sailor missing the ability to binge-watch Netflix, I have missed the ability to lose myself in the holy surroundings of a dedicated place of worship, steeped in history, candles lit demonstrating someone has prayed there, and the vague smell of incense signifying worship has recently taken place there.

When I was sea-going, I would take the opportunity to visit a church when alongside in a foreign port. I knew the importance of receiving from others in order to lead others in receiving. On one visit to Iceland, I went to the Catholic cathedral and afterwards noticed a change in myself. Just as others need to drink or sit in a swimming pool to rejuvenate, as a priest I need to receive the Holy Eucharist and the spiritual direction of others. Once I switched from seagoer to shore based, I had ample opportunity to visit other churches. It is considered poor form according to the customs of the Church of England to visit a previous parish; but I did find a new church where I could go and participate as one of the congregation rather than officiate as a priest, and it's refreshing. My first year in the Royal Navy taught me more about myself and my ministry than six years in a parish setting, that is, the importance of receiving and leading.

Prayer life

A common phrase that I heard throughout training, from serving and experienced RN chaplains, is 'the importance of a personal prayer life'. As a sea goer, you are very much isolated in that there aren't always others you can go to for support, pray with, or share concerns with. A personal prayer life is essential for all those who feel called to priestly ministry, but not everyone has a perfect prayer life. Mine is pretty mixed but almost always private. I am not very good with praying at specific times or for particular durations. I tend to pray more sporadically unless I attend communal prayers with colleagues. I pray when I am moved to pray, at the sound of a siren, after meeting with someone, when I need God's support.

At sea, I adopted a pattern of publicly and privately praying. Publicly, morning or evening prayer was often said alone. Still, when I thought no one was coming, I would suddenly be joined by someone who wanted to participate or was curious about what these prayer services involved. I quickly developed a more structured prayer life because it was my support system. I could lay my concerns, anxieties, and homesickness before God in prayer. In prayer, I sought God's guidance on how to deal with a specific person or situation, seeking strength to continue my ministry or for safety in times of uncertainty. Although I am not there solely as an embarked chaplain for religious purposes, I am God's representative onboard. My daily prayers were for the individual departments, for safe transit through rough seas, and for the enemies who would wish us harm. I would put prayer services on daily orders, not to attract a large audience but to remind the ship's company that I was praying for them. It quickly became apparent that the ship's company noticed this, and regularly I would be asked to remember family members in my prayers.

A prayer life is so important, not just for my own well-being and support but also for all those onboard. It was my prayer life that got me through the tough times, as well as help from family and friends ashore. My prayer life energised me daily and comforted me in times of loneliness or tiredness. Some who did not want to join me in prayer still relied upon my prayer life and felt reassured that they or their families were being prayed for. As a result, my prayer life changed from primarily public prayer for others to mostly private and more personal prayer. This pattern has continued with me and led to my exploration of Benedictine monasticism. St Benedict's view on prayer was that if you can only pray for a minute, pray for a minute. The focus of prayer is on God and, if your mind wanders because you are trying to spend an hour in prayer, then it loses its point. So pray for a minute, but pray often, that is my prayer life.

In the Holy Land, I also discovered the significance of praying the rosary. A pattern I adopt at sea is to say the chaplet of divine mercy every Sunday evening, alone, after leading the Holy Eucharist.

The times of isolation at sea have developed my prayer life, which I was not expecting. The opportunity not to rush from one meeting to the next, the chance to take myself off and to have times of silence and reflection. A disciplined prayer life with regular reflection is essential as a chaplain, especially when you are at sea. I have been pleasantly surprised how time at sea can be almost like a retreat and really strengthen my faith, my desire for prayerfulness and my ministry.

Am I separated from the church?

As a parish priest, I was employed and paid by the Diocese of Exeter. On joining the military as a chaplain, I was no longer employed by the 'church' but by the government, paid for by taxpayer's money. There is often a misconception that chaplains 'leave' the church when they become chaplains, but this isn't true. I am still active in my diocese with PTO (permission to officiate – given by the Bishop, allowing me to preach and preside in local parishes), and I attend clergy Chapter meetings as much as possible. Once my time in the Royal Navy is finished, I will return to parish ministry (but I will explore this more in the next chapter). In this way, I am not separate from the church but still a part of it, just exercising a ministry mainly for the 'unchurched' rather than the 'churched'.

Choosing to serve in the armed forces, some would consider my ministry as war-mongering and wrong, serving those who are effectively paid to fight and kill. Arguably, although a chaplain is a non-combatant, we are employed to maintain morale and enable operational capability so that sailors can defend and protect the nation's interests when required to do so. There will be many who consider war to be wrong but I have yet to meet a single military chaplain who believes that war is a part of God's plan.

Without a shadow of a doubt, I wish we lived in a world where war did not exist, where there were no such things as 'enemies' or the need to use force. However, I do believe that a peaceful world will one day exist and that is in heaven. Until then, I serve not just those who are employed potentially to take life in combat but also those who provide: humanitarian aid and disaster relief around the world; protection of global shipping lanes and the ships that we rely upon to fill the shelves in our supermarkets and transport parts for our everyday devices; those who help to keep drugs off our streets, and those who rush to the aid of those in times of crisis. The Royal Navy is not just functional and present for war. At times, war is the focus and use of its resources and abilities, but it also has a significant role in times of peace. In times of peace and war, I am proud to serve those who serve our country and very much feel that God has called me to this place.

So, in answer to my question, 'am I separated from the church?', the answer is both no and yes. No, I am still very much a part of the wider church and continue to serve God as a priest. But also, yes, in that some parts, or should I say people, of the church would not agree with my ministry due to its presence in times of war.

In my ministry so far with the Royal Navy, there have been times when I have grown as a Christian and a priest and times I have struggled to feel spiritually fulfilled or sustained. There have been times when I have been surrounded by like-minded priests who have supported me and times when I have felt isolated and alone. However, above all, I have always felt the presence of God guiding, supporting, and sustaining me. As a result, my priestly ministry, faith, and spirituality have not just been maintained during service as a chaplain in the Royal Navy but expanded, deepened, and enhanced.

11

End ex

This chapter is the last and the shortest of all chapters in this book, partly because I have yet to think this far ahead. However, here is a brief insight for those wondering what it might look like when you come to the end of your time serving as a chaplain in the Royal Navy.

Your service in the armed forces comes to an end once you reach your termination date (TX date), that is, the date on which your commission of service ends, you are discharged medically, you are discharged for committing an offence or your 'services are no longer required', or you submit notice to leave. All armed forces members must give twelve months' notice to leave if they wish to leave the service before their time is served. For some branches, there is a return of service, that is, you must do a minimum number of years before you are entitled to put in your notice to leave. However, for chaplains, there is not usually any return of service, meaning you can put in your notice to leave at any stage. To submit your notice to leave is quite simple, with just a few clicks of the mouse. After you have submitted notice to leave, and subject to being eligible, there is an interview to determine why you want to leave and if anything can be done to encourage you to stay, before the countdown begins until you return to 'civvie street' or 'go outside'.

After submitting notice to leave, or when you are coming to the end of your commission, resettlement benefits will kick in. These benefits vary depending on how long you have served. But they usually include: support in interview practice and CV writing; time off to apply for jobs and attend interviews, and financial aid to complete courses to help you when you leave the forces. It is possible to be released quicker than 12 months, but this depends on the needs of the service and if you have a job to go to.

Chaplains will most likely return to a parish after leaving the military. Depending on when they joined, they may have only decided to spend six years in service. Although it is common for clergy to join the Royal Navy as chaplains and to remain with the Royal Navy for as long as possible, it does not need to be this way. A Parish Priest could join the Royal Navy and serve for six or more years as they would in a parish, returning to parish ministry with the benefit of all the experiences they have had in their military service.

What does my future look like? I don't know. I am often asked how long I will serve in the Royal Navy as a chaplain. My answer is usually *'as long as God wants me to'* or *'for as long as I am useful'*.

The reality is that it will be one of three reasons that I will leave the Royal Navy:

1. My wife decides that she has had enough of me being away and asks me to leave (she has the 'seven clicks' grenade, since part of the deal of me joining was, when she says she can't do it anymore, I submit notice to leave).
2. God calls me to another ministry.
3. I reach my termination (TX) date.

You may have noticed that none of those three options include me choosing to put my notice in or declining an extension to service, and that is because I love what I do. From the very start, I have found this unique ministry utterly amazing. I spend my days doing predominately pastoral ministry, walking alongside people from various backgrounds, sometimes being asked to share my faith and sometimes to baptise or marry. I spend my days actively seeing God at work in others from unchurched backgrounds and have real adventures with people with whom I become close friends. I will return to parish ministry one day, and I will return with a vast amount of experience of working with young people, people in crisis, people from a wide range of backgrounds and cultures. I will return with experiences and adventures that have taught me much about God and about myself.

I started writing this book wondering if I would ever finish it or what I would do with it. But if you have made it this far, I hope it has been helpful. If you are exploring a vocation to military chaplaincy, all I can say is that, if you feel called to it, it will transform your life and you will also have a part in transforming others' lives.

To all those who find themselves at sea right now and those who will find themselves at sea in the future, fair winds and following seas...